AWS Certified Advanced Networking - Specialty ANS-C01 Exam Preparation

INTRODUCTION:

Achieve **success** in your **AWS Certified Advanced Networking - Specialty ANS-C01 Exam** on the **first try** with our **new** and **exclusive preparation book.**

This **comprehensive resource** is **designed** to **help you test** your **knowledge, providing** a **collection** of the **latest questions** with **detailed explanations** and **official references.**

Save both **time** and **money** by **investing in this book**, which **covers all the topics included** in the **AWS Certified Advanced Networking - Specialty ANS-C01 exam.**

This **book** includes **two full-length, highly important practice tests, each** with **65 questions,** for a **total** of **130 questions.** It also provides **detailed explanations** for **each question** and **official reference links.**

Dedicate your **effort** to **mastering** these **AWS Certified Advanced Networking - Specialty ANS-C01 exam questions,** as they **offer up-to-date information** on the **entire exam syllabus.**

This book is **strategically crafted** to not only assess your **knowledge** and **skills** but also to **boost your confidence for the real exam.**

With a focus on **thorough preparation, passing** the **official AWS Certified Advanced Networking - Specialty ANS-C01 Exam** on your **first attempt becomes achievable** through **diligent study of these valuable resources.**

The AWS Certified Advanced Networking - Specialty (ANS-

C01) exam has a total of **65 questions.** However, there's a breakdown to consider:

50 scored questions: These questions directly affect your pass/ fail outcome.

15 unscored questions: These are used by AWS to evaluate potential future exam questions and don't influence your score.

So, while you'll see 65 questions during the exam, only **50 of them will determine if you pass.**

Welcome!

PRACTICE TEST I

1) A company is planning to develop a service requiring encryption during data transmission. The data must remain encrypted between the client and the backend without any decryption in transit. The service will utilize the gRPC protocol over TCP port 443 and must be capable of handling thousands of simultaneous connections. The backend will be hosted on an Amazon Elastic Kubernetes Service (Amazon EKS) cluster, which will be equipped with both the Kubernetes Cluster Autoscaler and the Horizontal Pod Autoscaler. Additionally, the company needs to implement mutual TLS for two-way authentication between the client and the backend. Which solution will meet these requirements?

A. Install the AWS Load Balancer Controller for Kubernetes. Using that controller, configure a Network Load Balancer with a TCP listener on port 443 to forward traffic to the IP addresses of the backend service Pods.

B. Install the AWS Load Balancer Controller for Kubernetes. Configure an Application Load Balancer with an HTTPS listener on port 443 using the controller to forward traffic to the backend service Pods' IP addresses.

C. Create a target group and add the EKS managed node group's Auto Scaling group as a target. Create an Application Load Balancer with an HTTPS listener on port 443 to forward traffic to the target group.

D. Create a target group and add the EKS managed node group's

Auto Scaling group as a target. Create a Network Load Balancer with a TLS listener on port 443 to forward traffic to the target group.

2) A company is deploying a new application in the AWS Cloud. They require a highly available web server positioned behind an Elastic Load Balancer. The load balancer should route requests to multiple target groups based on the URL in the request. All traffic must use HTTPS, with TLS processing offloaded to the load balancer. Additionally, the web server must capture the user's IP address to maintain accurate logs for security purposes. Which solution will meet these requirements?

A. Deploy an Application Load Balancer with an HTTPS listener. Implement path-based routing rules to direct traffic to the appropriate target group. Ensure the X-Forwarded-For request header is included with traffic sent to the targets.

B. Deploy an Application Load Balancer with an HTTPS listener for each domain. Implement host-based routing rules to direct traffic to the appropriate target group for each domain. Ensure the X-Forwarded-For request header is included with traffic sent to the targets.

C. Deploy a Network Load Balancer with a TLS listener. Implement path-based routing rules to direct traffic to the appropriate target group. Configure client IP address preservation for traffic sent to the targets.

D. Deploy a Network Load Balancer with a TLS listener for each domain. Implement host-based routing rules to direct traffic to the appropriate target group for each domain. Configure client IP address preservation for traffic sent to the targets.

3) A company has developed an AWS-based application to track inventory levels of vending machines and automatically initiate the restocking process. The company intends to integrate this application with vending machines and deploy these machines in various markets worldwide. The application is hosted in a VPC within the us-east-1 Region and comprises an Amazon Elastic Container Service (Amazon ECS) cluster behind an Application Load Balancer (ALB). Communication between the vending machines and the application occurs over HTTPS.

The company plans to use an AWS Global Accelerator and configure the accelerator's static IP addresses in the vending machines for accessing the application endpoint. The application must only be accessible via the accelerator, preventing direct internet connections to the ALB endpoint. Which solution will meet these requirements?

A. Configure the ALB in a private subnet of the VPC. Attach an internet gateway without adding routes in the subnet route tables to point to the internet gateway. Configure the accelerator with endpoint groups that include the ALB endpoint. Configure the ALB's security group to only allow inbound traffic from the internet on the ALB listener port.

B. Place the ALB in a private subnet of the VPC. Configure the accelerator with endpoint groups that include the ALB endpoint. Set the ALB's security group to allow inbound traffic only from the internet on the ALB listener port.

C. Place the ALB in a public subnet of the VPC. Attach an internet gateway. Add routes in the subnet route tables pointing to the internet gateway. Configure the accelerator with endpoint groups that include the ALB endpoint. Set the ALB's security group to allow inbound traffic only from the accelerator's IP addresses on the ALB listener port.

D. Place the ALB in a private subnet of the VPC. Attach an internet gateway. Add routes in the subnet route tables pointing to the internet gateway. Configure the accelerator with endpoint groups that include the ALB endpoint. Set the ALB's security group to allow inbound traffic only from the accelerator's IP addresses on the ALB listener port.

4) A global delivery company is updating its fleet management system. The company consists of multiple business units, each responsible for designing and maintaining applications hosted in its own AWS account. These applications reside in separate VPCs within the same AWS Region. Each business unit's applications are configured to retrieve data from a central shared services VPC. The company seeks a network connectivity architecture that offers detailed security controls and can scale to accommodate additional business units accessing data from the central shared services VPC in the future. Which solution will meet these requirements in the MOST secure manner?

A. Establish a central transit gateway and attach it to each application VPC, enabling full mesh connectivity between all VPCs.

B. Set up VPC peering connections between the central shared services VPC and each application VPC in every business unit's AWS account.

C. Create VPC endpoint services powered by AWS PrivateLink in the central shared services VPCreate VPC endpoints in each application VPC.

D. Deploy a central transit VPC with a VPN appliance from AWS Marketplace, and establish VPN attachments from each VPC to the transit VPC, enabling full mesh connectivity among all VPCs.

5) A company utilizes a 4 Gbps AWS Direct Connect dedicated connection with a link aggregation group (LAG) bundle to connect to five VPCs deployed in the us-east-1 Region. Each VPC caters to a different business unit and employs its private VIF for connectivity to the on-premises environment. Users are experiencing sluggishness when accessing resources hosted on AWS.

A network engineer detects periodic spikes in throughput, saturating the Direct Connect connection for approximately an hour each business day. The company seeks to identify the business unit responsible for these spikes and implement a solution to address the issue. Which solution will meet these requirements?

A. Review the Amazon CloudWatch metrics for VirtualInterfaceBpsEgress and VirtualInterfaceBpsIngress to determine which VIF is sending the highest throughput during the period in which slowness is observed. Create a new 10 Gbps dedicated connection. Shift traffic from the existing dedicated connection to the new dedicated connection.

B. Analyze the Amazon CloudWatch metrics for VirtualInterfaceBpsEgress and VirtualInterfaceBpsIngress to identify the VIF with the highest throughput during the slow period. Upgrade the bandwidth of the current dedicated connection to 10 Gbps.

C. Examine the Amazon CloudWatch metrics for ConnectionBpsIngress and ConnectionPpsEgress to determine the VIF with the highest throughput during the slow period. Upgrade the existing dedicated connection to a 5 Gbps hosted connection.

D. Examine the Amazon CloudWatch metrics for ConnectionBpsIngress and ConnectionPpsEgress to identify the VIF with the highest throughput during the slow period. Establish a new 10 Gbps dedicated connection and transfer traffic from the existing connection to the new one.

6) A software-as-a-service (SaaS) provider hosts its solution on Amazon EC2 instances within an AWS Cloud-based VPC. All customers of the provider also have their environments in the AWS Cloud.

During a recent design meeting, it was discovered that customers have IP addresses that overlap with the provider's AWS deployment. The customers have expressed that they are unwilling to share their internal IP addresses and prefer not to connect to the provider's SaaS service over the internet. Which combination of steps is part of a solution that meets these requirements? (Choose two.)

A. Deploy the SaaS service endpoint behind a Network Load Balancer.

B. Configure an endpoint service, and grant the customers permission to create a connection to the endpoint service.

C. Deploy the SaaS service endpoint behind an Application Load Balancer.

D. Configure a VPC peering connection to the customer VPCs. Route traffic through NAT gateways.

E. Deploy an AWS Transit Gateway, and connect the SaaS VPC to it. Share the transit gateway with the customers. Configure routing on the transit gateway.

7) A network engineer is architecting the infrastructure

for a healthcare company's workload transition to the AWS Cloud. The design mandates that all data exchanged with the on-premises environment be encrypted during transit. Furthermore, all traffic must undergo inspection within the cloud prior to being permitted to exit to the on-premises environment or the internet.

The company plans to make certain components of the workload accessible via the internet for patients to schedule appointments. The architecture needs to secure these components and defend them against DDoS attacks. Additionally, the architecture must mitigate financial liability for services that expand during a DDoS incident.

Which combination of steps should the network engineer take to meet all these requirements for the workload? (Choose three.)

A. Use Traffic Mirroring to copy all traffic to a fleet of traffic capture appliances.

B. Set up AWS WAF on all network components.

C. Configure an AWS Lambda function to create Deny rules in security groups to block malicious IP addresses.

D. Use AWS Direct Connect with MACsec support for connectivity to the cloud.

E. Use Gateway Load Balancers to insert third-party firewalls for inline traffic inspection.

F. Configure AWS Shield Advanced and ensure that it is configured on all public assets.

8) A retail company is operating its service on AWS. The architecture incorporates Application Load Balancers (ALBs) located in public subnets. The ALB target groups are set

up to route traffic to backend Amazon EC2 instances situated in private subnets. These backend EC2 instances can communicate with externally hosted services over the internet through a NAT gateway.

The company has observed a notable increase in NAT gateway usage in its billing. A network engineer must identify the cause of this surge in usage.

Which options can the network engineer use to investigate the traffic through the NAT gateway? (Choose two.)

A. Enable VPC flow logs on the NAT gateway's elastic network interface. Publish the logs to a log group in Amazon CloudWatch Logs. Use CloudWatch Logs Insights to query and analyze the logs.

B. Enable NAT gateway access logs. Publish the logs to a log group in Amazon CloudWatch Logs. Use CloudWatch Logs Insights to query and analyze the logs.

C. Configure Traffic Mirroring on the NAT gateway's elastic network interface. Send the traffic to an additional EC2 instance. Use tools such as tcpdump and Wireshark to query and analyze the mirrored traffic.

D. Enable VPC flow logs on the NAT gateway's elastic network interface. Publish the logs to an Amazon S3 bucket. Create a custom table for the S3 bucket in Amazon Athena to describe the log structure. Use Athena to query and analyze the logs.

E. Enable NAT gateway access logs. Publish the logs to an Amazon S3 bucket. Create a custom table for the S3 bucket in Amazon Athena to describe the log structure. Use Athena to query and analyze the logs.

9) A banking company is running its public mobile banking

stack on AWS with deployments in a VPC featuring both private and public subnets, using IPv4 networking exclusively. The company has chosen to adopt a third-party service provider's API, which mandates IPv6 compatibility, necessitating integration with the existing environment. The service provider's API requires the use of IPv6.

A network engineer is tasked with enabling IPv6 connectivity for an existing workload deployed in a private subnet. The company's policy prohibits IPv6 traffic from the public internet and requires that the company's servers initiate all IPv6 connectivity. The engineer enables IPv6 in the VPC and private subnets accordingly.

Which solution will meet these requirements?

A. Create an internet gateway and a NAT gateway in the VPC. Add a route to the existing subnet route tables to point IPv6 traffic to the NAT gateway.

B. Create an internet gateway and a NAT instance in the VPC. Add a route to the existing subnet route tables to point IPv6 traffic to the NAT instance.

C. Create an egress-only Internet gateway in the VPAdd a route to the existing subnet route tables to point IPv6 traffic to the egress-only internet gateway.

D. Create an egress-only internet gateway in the VPC. Configure a security group that denies all inbound traffic. Associate the security group with the egress-only internet gateway.

10) A company has installed an AWS Network Firewall in a VPC. A network engineer must devise a solution to swiftly deliver Network Firewall flow logs to the company's Amazon OpenSearch Service (Amazon Elasticsearch Service) cluster.

Which solution will meet these requirements?

A. Establish an Amazon S3 bucket and an AWS Lambda function to load logs into the Amazon OpenSearch Service (Amazon Elasticsearch Service) cluster. Enable Amazon Simple Notification Service (Amazon SNS) notifications on the S3 bucket to trigger the Lambda function. Configure flow logs for the firewall and designate the S3 bucket as the destination.

B. Create an Amazon Kinesis Data Firehose delivery stream that includes the Amazon OpenSearch Service (Amazon Elasticsearch Service) cluster as the destination. Configure flow logs for the firewall Set the Kinesis Data Firehose delivery stream as the destination for the Network Firewall flow logs.

C. Configure flow logs for the firewall and set the Amazon OpenSearch Service (Amazon Elasticsearch Service) cluster as the destination for the Network Firewall flow logs.

D. Establish an Amazon Kinesis data stream with the Amazon OpenSearch Service (Amazon Elasticsearch Service) cluster as the target. Configure flow logs for the firewall and designate the Kinesis data stream as the destination for the Network Firewall flow logs.

11) A company is utilizing custom DNS servers running BIND for name resolution within its VPCs. These VPCs are spread across multiple AWS accounts that belong to the same organization within AWS Organizations. All VPCs are connected to a transit gateway. The BIND servers are situated in a central VPC and are set up to forward all queries for an on-premises DNS domain to DNS servers hosted in an on-premises data center. To ensure that all VPCs utilize the custom DNS servers, a network engineer has configured a VPC DHCP options set in all VPCs, specifying the custom DNS servers to be used as domain name servers.

Multiple development teams within the company require access to Amazon Elastic File System (Amazon EFS). One of the development teams has created a new EFS file system but is unable to mount it to an Amazon EC2 instance. Upon investigation, the network engineer determines that the EC2 instance cannot resolve the IP address for the EFS mount point fs-33444567d.efs.us-east-1.amazonaws.com. The network engineer must implement a solution to enable all development teams in the organization to mount EFS file systems.

Which combination of steps will meet these requirements? (Choose two.)

A. Configure the BIND DNS servers in the central VPC to forward queries for efs.us-east-1.amazonaws.com to the Amazon provided DNS server (169.254.169.253).

B. Create an Amazon Route 53 Resolver outbound endpoint in the central VPC. Update all the VPC DHCP options sets to use AmazonProvidedDNS for name resolution.

C. Create an Amazon Route 53 Resolver inbound endpoint in the central VPUpdate all the VPC DHCP options sets to use the Route 53 Resolver inbound endpoint in the central VPC for name resolution.

D. Create an Amazon Route 53 Resolver rule to forward queries for the on-premises domain to the on-premises DNS servers. Share the rule with the organization by using AWS Resource Access Manager (AWS RAM). Associate the rule with all the VPCs.

E. Create an Amazon Route 53 private hosted zone for the efs.us-east-1.amazonaws.com domain. Associate the private hosted zone with the VPC where the EC2 instance is deployed. Create an A record for fs-33444567d.efs.us-east-1.amazonaws.com in the private hosted zone. Configure the A record to return the mount target of the EFS mount point.

12) An ecommerce company hosts a web application on Amazon EC2 instances to manage fluctuating customer demand. These instances are integrated into an Auto Scaling group. The company seeks to establish a method for directing customer traffic to the EC2 instances while ensuring that all traffic is encrypted throughout, without any decryption at intermediate points.

Which solution will meet these requirements?

A. Create an Application Load Balancer (ALB). Add an HTTPS listener to the ALB. Configure the Auto Scaling group to register instances with the ALB's target group.

B. Create an Amazon CloudFront distribution. Configure the distribution with a custom SSL/TLS certificate. Set the Auto Scaling group as the distribution's origin.

C. Create a Network Load Balancer (NLB). Add a TCP listener to the NLB. Configure the Auto Scaling group to register instances with the NLB's target group.

D. Create a Gateway Load Balancer (GLB). Configure the Auto Scaling group to register instances with the GLB's target group.

13) A company operates two on-premises data centers, each equipped with a company-managed router. Both data centers are connected to an AWS Direct Connect gateway through private virtual interfaces, with dedicated connections. The router at the first location advertises 110 routes to the Direct Connect gateway using BGP, while the router at the second location advertises 60 routes. The Direct Connect gateway is linked to a company VPC through a virtual private gateway.

A network engineer receives reports of unreachable resources in the VPC from various locations in both data centers.

Upon inspecting the VPC route table, the engineer notices that routes from the first data center location are not being populated into the route table. The network engineer must resolve this issue with the utmost operational efficiency.

What should the network engineer do to meet these requirements?

A. Remove the Direct Connect gateway, and create a new private virtual interface from each company router to the virtual private gateway of the VPC.

B. Change the router configurations to summarize the advertised routes.

C. Open a support ticket to increase the quota on advertised routes to the VPC route table.

D. Create an AWS Transit Gateway. Attach the transit gateway to the VPC, and connect the Direct Connect gateway to the transit gateway.

14) The company has extended its network into the AWS Cloud through a hybrid architecture involving multiple AWS accounts. A shared AWS account has been established for connectivity to on-premises data centers and company offices. Workloads include private web-based services for internal use, running in various AWS accounts. Office-based employees access these services using a DNS name within an on-premises DNS zone named example.internal.

The current process for registering a new service running on AWS involves a manual and complex change request to the internal DNS, requiring coordination among multiple teams.

The company aims to simplify the DNS registration process by granting service creators access to register their DNS records.

The network engineer must design a solution that achieves this goal, prioritizing cost-effectiveness and minimizing the need for configuration changes.

Which combination of steps should the network engineer take to meet these requirements? (Choose three.)

A. Create a record for each service in its local private hosted zone (serviceA.account1.aws.example.internal). Provide this DNS record to the employees who need access.

B. Create an Amazon Route 53 Resolver inbound endpoint in the shared account VPC. Create a conditional forwarder for a domain named aws.example.internal on the on-premises DNS servers. Set the forwarding IP addresses to the inbound endpoint's IP addresses that were created.

C. Create an Amazon Route 53 Resolver rule to forward any queries made to onprem.example.internal to the on-premises DNS servers.

D. Create an Amazon Route 53 private hosted zone named aws.example.internal in the shared AWS account to resolve queries for this domain.

E. Launch two Amazon EC2 instances in the shared AWS account. Install BIND on each instance. Create a DNS conditional forwarder on each BIND server to forward queries for each subdomain under aws.example.internal to the appropriate private hosted zone in each AWS account. Create a conditional forwarder for a domain named aws.example.internal on the on-premises DNS servers. Set the forwarding IP addresses to the IP addresses of the BIND servers.

F. Create a private hosted zone in the shared AWS account for each account that runs the service. Configure the private hosted zone to contain aws.example.internal in the domain (account1.aws.example.internal). Associate the private hosted zone with the VPC that runs the service and the shared account VPC.

15) A company with multiple AWS accounts, each containing one or more VPCs, has implemented a new security requirement to inspect all traffic between VPCs. The company has deployed a transit gateway to facilitate connectivity between all VPCs. Additionally, a shared services VPC has been established with Amazon EC2 instances hosting IDS services for stateful inspection. These EC2 instances are spread across three Availability Zones. VPC associations and routing have been configured on the transit gateway. As part of the migration process, the company has moved several test VPCs to the new solution for traffic inspection.

Soon after the configuration of routing, the company receives reports of intermittent connections for traffic that crosses Availability Zones.

What should a network engineer do to resolve this issue?

A. Modify the transit gateway VPC attachment on the shared services VPC by enabling cross-Availability Zone load balancing.

B. Modify the transit gateway VPC attachment on the shared services VPC by enabling appliance mode support.

C. Modify the transit gateway by selecting VPN equal-cost multi-path (ECMP) routing support.

D. Modify the transit gateway by selecting multicast support.

16) After a security audit, a company operating in the us-west-2 Region needs to eliminate its use of a NAT gateway, which was providing internet connectivity for private subnets within a VPC.

The network engineer needs to devise a solution to ensure that resources in the private subnets, which utilize the unified Amazon CloudWatch agent, can continue to function properly following the removal of the NAT gateway.

Which combination of steps should the network engineer take to meet these requirements? (Choose three.)

A. Validate that private DNS is enabled on the VPC by setting the enableDnsHostnames VPC attribute and the enableDnsSupport VPC attribute to true.

B. Create a new security group with an entry to allow outbound traffic that uses the TCP protocol on port 443 to destination 0.0.0.0/0

C. Create a new security group with entries to allow inbound traffic that uses the TCP protocol on port 443 from the IP prefixes of the private subnets.

D. Create the following interface VPC endpoints in the VPC: com.amazonaws.us-west-2.logs and com.amazonaws.us-west-2.monitoring. Associate the new security group with the endpoint network interfaces.

E. Create the following interface VPC endpoint in the VPC: com.amazonaws.us-west-2.cloudwatch. Associate the new security group with the endpoint network interfaces.

F. Associate the VPC endpoint or endpoints with route tables that the private subnets use.

17) An international company specializing in tsunami early warning plans to deploy IoT devices for monitoring sea waves globally. Data from these devices must swiftly reach the company's AWS infrastructure. The company operates three global operation centers, each with its AWS Direct Connect

connection. Additionally, each center connects to the internet through at least two upstream internet service providers.

The company utilizes its own provider-independent (PI) address space. The IoT devices utilize TCP protocols to ensure the reliable transmission of the data they collect. These devices have access to both landline and mobile internet connectivity. The infrastructure and solution will be deployed across multiple AWS Regions. Amazon Route 53 will be utilized for DNS services. A network engineer needs to design connectivity between the IoT devices and the services that run in the AWS Cloud.

Which solution will meet these requirements with the HIGHEST availability?

A. Set up an Amazon CloudFront distribution with origin failover. Create an origin group for each Region where the solution is deployed.

B. Set up Route 53 latency-based routing. Add latency alias records. For the latency alias records, set the value of Evaluate Target Health to Yes.

C. Set up an accelerator in AWS Global Accelerator. Configure Regional endpoint groups and health checks.

D. Set up Bring Your Own IP (BYOIP) addresses. Use the same PI addresses for each Region where the solution is deployed.

18) A company is preparing to migrate its critical workloads from an on-premises data center to Amazon EC2 instances. The migration plan involves establishing a new 10 Gbps AWS Direct Connect dedicated connection from the on-premises data center to a VPC connected to a transit gateway. All data transfers during the migration will be encrypted between the on-premises data center and the AWS Cloud.

Which solution will meet these requirements while providing the HIGHEST throughput?

A. Configure a public VIF on the Direct Connect connection. Configure an AWS Site-to-Site VPN connection to the transit gateway as a VPN attachment.

B. Configure a transit VIF on the Direct Connect connection. Configure an IPsec VPN connection to an EC2 instance that is running third-party VPN software.

C. Configure MACsec for the Direct Connect connection. Configure a transit VIF to a Direct Connect gateway that is associated with the transit gateway.

D. Configure a public VIF on the Direct Connect connection. Configure two AWS Site-to-Site VPN connections to the transit gateway. Enable equal-cost multi-path (ECMP) routing.

19) A network engineer is tasked with creating an AWS CloudFormation template to provision a virtual private gateway, a customer gateway, a VPN connection, and static routes in a route table. While testing the template, the network engineer observes that an error has occurred, causing the CloudFormation stack to roll back.

What should the network engineer do to resolve the error?

A. Change the order of resource creation in the CloudFormation template.

B. Add the DependsOn attribute to the resource declaration for the virtual private gateway. Specify the route table entry resource.

C. Add a wait condition in the template to wait for the creation of the virtual private gateway.

D. Add the DependsOn attribute to the resource declaration for the route table entry. Specify the virtual private gateway resource.

20) A company utilizes a hybrid infrastructure for its IT services, operating across multiple sites. The company deploys resources on AWS in the us-east-1 Region and in the eu-west-2 Region, as well as in its own data centers located in the United States (US) and the United Kingdom (UK). In both AWS Regions, the company employs a transit gateway to interconnect 15 VPCs. Additionally, the company has established a transit gateway peering connection between the two transit gateways. The VPC CIDR blocks are non-overlapping and can be aggregated either on a Regional level or for the entire AWS environment.

The data centers are linked via a private WAN connection, with dynamic IP routing information exchanged through Interior BGP (iBGP) sessions. Connectivity to AWS is maintained by each data center through a dedicated AWS Direct Connect connection in the US and UK. Each Direct Connect connection terminates on a Direct Connect gateway and is linked to a local transit gateway through a transit VIF.

Traffic is routed along the shortest geographical path from source to destination. For instance, packets from the UK data center destined for resources in the eu-west-2 Region travel via the local Direct Connect connection. For cross-Region data transfers, such as from the UK data center to VPCs in us-east-1, the private WAN connection is utilized to minimize costs on AWS. Each transit gateway association on the Direct Connect gateway is configured by the network engineer to advertise VPC-specific CIDR IP prefixes only from the local Region. Routes to the other Region are learned through BGP from the routers in the other data center in their original, non-aggregated form.

The company faced challenges with cross-Region data transfers due to problems with its private WAN connection. The network engineer must adjust the routing configuration to avoid similar disruptions in the future without altering the original traffic routing objective when the network is functioning normally.

Which modifications will meet these requirements? (Choose two.)

A. Remove all the VPC CIDR prefixes from the list of subnets advertised through the local Direct Connect connection. Add the company's entire AWS environment aggregate route to the list of subnets advertised through the local Direct Connect connection.

B. Add the CIDR prefixes from the other Region VPCs and the local VPC CIDR blocks to the list of subnets advertised through the local Direct Connect connection. Configure data center routers to make routing decisions based on the BGP communities received.

C. Add the aggregate IP prefix for the other Region and the local VPC CIDR blocks to the list of subnets advertised through the local Direct Connect connection.

D. Add the aggregate IP prefix for the company's entire AWS environment and the local VPC CIDR blocks to the list of subnets advertised through the local Direct Connect connection.

E. Remove all the VPC CIDR prefixes from the list of subnets advertised through the local Direct Connect connection. Add both Regional aggregate IP prefixes to the list of subnets advertised through the Direct Connect connection on both sides of the network. Configure data center routers to make routing decisions based on the BGP communities received.

21) A network engineer is tasked with designing a new

solution to detect and troubleshoot network anomalies. The engineer has enabled Traffic Mirroring, but the mirrored traffic is overloading the Amazon EC2 instance serving as the traffic mirror target. This EC2 instance hosts tools used by the company's security team to analyze the traffic. The engineer seeks to design a highly available solution capable of scaling to accommodate the increased demand of the mirrored traffic.

Which solution will meet these requirements?

A. Deploy a Network Load Balancer (NLB) as the traffic mirror target. Behind the NLB. deploy a fleet of EC2 instances in an Auto Scaling group. Use Traffic Mirroring as necessary.

B. Deploy an Application Load Balancer (ALB) as the traffic mirror target. Behind the ALB, deploy a fleet of EC2 instances in an Auto Scaling group. Use Traffic Mirroring only during non-business hours.

C. Deploy a Gateway Load Balancer (GLB) as the traffic mirror target. Behind the GLB. deploy a fleet of EC2 instances in an Auto Scaling group. Use Traffic Mirroring as necessary.

D. Deploy an Application Load Balancer (ALB) with an HTTPS listener as the traffic mirror target. Behind the ALB. deploy a fleet of EC2 instances in an Auto Scaling group. Use Traffic Mirroring only during active events or business hours.

22) A company with a hybrid architecture has established an AWS Direct Connect connection between its on-premises data center and AWS. The company hosts production applications in both environments, with on-premises applications using the domain name corp.example.com, and VPC applications hosted under the domain aws.example.com in an Amazon Route 53 private hosted zone. These applications require communication between the on-premises and VPC

environments.

The company employs an open-source recursive DNS resolver within a VPC subnet and a DNS resolver in the on-premises data center. The on-premises DNS resolver is configured with a forwarder to direct requests for the aws.example.com domain to the VPC's DNS resolver. Conversely, the VPC's DNS resolver is configured with a forwarder to direct requests for the corp.example.com domain to the on-premises DNS resolver. The company has decided to substitute the open-source recursive DNS resolver with Amazon Route 53 Resolver endpoints.

Which combination of steps should a network engineer take to make this replacement? (Choose three.)

A. Create a Route 53 Resolver rule to forward aws.example.com domain queries to the IP addresses of the outbound endpoint.

B. Configure the on-premises DNS resolver to forward aws.example.com domain queries to the IP addresses of the inbound endpoint.

C. Create a Route 53 Resolver inbound endpoint and a Route 53 Resolver outbound endpoint.

D. Create a Route 53 Resolver rule to forward aws.example.com domain queries to the IP addresses of the inbound endpoint.

E. Create a Route 53 Resolver rule to forward corp.example.com domain queries to the IP address of the on-premises DNS resolver.

F. Configure the on-premises DNS resolver to forward aws.example.com queries to the IP addresses of the outbound endpoint.

23) A government contractor is architecting a multi-account

environment for a customer, featuring multiple VPCs. A network security policy mandates that all traffic moving between any two VPCs undergo transparent inspection by a third-party appliance.

The customer requires a solution leveraging AWS Transit Gateway, ensuring high availability across multiple Availability Zones with support for automated failover. Additionally, the solution must not allow for asymmetric routing with the inspection appliances.

Which combination of steps is part of a solution that meets these requirements? (Choose two.)

A. Deploy two clusters that consist of multiple appliances across multiple Availability Zones in a designated inspection VPC. Connect the inspection VPC to the transit gateway by using a VPC attachment. Create a target group, and register the appliances with the target group. Create a Network Load Balancer (NLB), and set it up to forward to the newly created target group. Configure a default route in the inspection VPCs transit gateway subnet toward the NLB.

B. Deploy two clusters that consist of multiple appliances across multiple Availability Zones in a designated inspection VPC. Connect the inspection VPC to the transit gateway by using a VPC attachment. Create a target group, and register the appliances with the target group. Create a Gateway Load Balancer, and set it up to forward to the newly created target group. Configure a default route in the inspection VPC's transit gateway subnet toward the Gateway Load Balancer endpoint.

C. Configure two route tables on the transit gateway. Associate one route table with all the attachments of the application VPCs. Associate the other route table with the inspection VPC's attachment. Propagate all VPC attachments into the inspection route table. Define a static default route in the application route table. Enable appliance mode on the attachment that connects the inspection VPC.

D. Configure two route tables on the transit gateway. Associate one route table with all the attachments of the application VPCs. Associate the other route table with the inspection VPCs attachment. Propagate all VPC attachments into the application route table. Define a static default route in the inspection route table. Enable appliance mode on the attachment that connects the inspection VPC.

E. Configure one route table on the transit gateway. Associate the route table with all the VPCs. Propagate all VPC attachments into the route table. Define a static default route in the route table.

24) A company has deployed Amazon EC2 instances within private subnets of a VPC. The EC2 instances are required to be the initiators of any outbound requests, including those to the company's on-premises data center via an AWS Direct Connect connection. Direct communication from resources outside the VPC to the EC2 instances is prohibited.

The customer gateway in the on-premises data center is configured with a stateful firewall device that filters incoming and outgoing requests to and from multiple VPCs. Furthermore, the company aims to utilize a single IP match rule to permit all communications from the EC2 instances to its data center via a single IP address.

Which solution will meet these requirements with the LEAST amount of operational overhead?

A. Establish a VPN connection through the Direct Connect connection using the on-premises firewall. Restrict all traffic from on-premises to AWS while permitting stateful connections initiated by the EC2 instances.

B. Configure the on-premises firewall to filter requests from the on-premises network to the EC2 instances, allowing stateful connections only if initiated by the EC2 instances in the VPC.

C. Deploy a NAT gateway into a private subnet in the VPC where the EC2 instances are deployed. Specify the NAT gateway type as private. Configure the on-premises firewall to allow connections from the IP address that is assigned to the NAT gateway.

D. Deploy a NAT instance in a private subnet within the VPC containing the EC2 instances. Configure the on-premises firewall to allow connections from the IP address assigned to the NAT instance.

25) A global company runs its non-production environments in three AWS Regions: eu-west-1, us-east-1, and us-west-1. The company hosts all production workloads in two on-premises data centers. With 60 AWS accounts, each account has two VPCs in every Region. Each VPC has a virtual private gateway, terminating two VPN connections for resilient connectivity to the data centers. This setup results in a total of 360 VPN tunnels to each data center, leading to significant management overhead. The maximum VPN throughput for each Region is 500 Mbps.

The company wants to migrate the production environments to AWS. The company needs a solution that will simplify the network architecture and allow for future growth. The production environments will generate an additional 2 Gbps of traffic per Region back to the data centers. This traffic will increase over time.

Which solution will meet these requirements?

A. Establish an AWS Direct Connect connection from each data center to AWS in all Regions. Create and link private VIFs to a single Direct Connect gateway. Connect the Direct Connect gateway to all VPCs. Remove existing VPN connections directly attached to the virtual private gateways.

B. Deploy a single transit gateway with VPN connections from each data center. Use AWS Resource Access Manager (AWS RAM) to share the transit gateway with each account. Attach the transit gateway to each VPC. Remove existing VPN connections directly attached to the virtual private gateways.

C. Create a transit gateway in each Region with multiple new VPN connections from each data center. Share the transit gateways with each account using AWS Resource Access Manager (AWS RAM). In each Region, connect the transit gateway to each VPC. Remove existing VPN connections directly attached to the virtual private gateways.

D. Establish peering between all VPCs in each Region and a new VPC that will serve as a centralized transit VPC. Create new VPN connections from each data center to the transit VPCs. Terminate the original VPN connections attached to all original VPCs. Maintain the new VPN connection to the new transit VPC in each Region.

26) A company is developing its website on AWS within a single VPC. The VPC contains both public and private subnets across two Availability Zones. The website includes static content such as images, which the company stores in Amazon S3.

The company has deployed a fleet of Amazon EC2 instances as web servers in a private subnet. These EC2 instances are part of an Auto Scaling group and are positioned behind an Application Load Balancer. The EC2 instances will handle incoming traffic and need to fetch content from an S3 bucket to display the webpages. The company uses AWS Direct Connect with a public VIF to enable on-premises connectivity to the S3 bucket.

A network engineer notices that traffic between the EC2 instances and Amazon S3 is routing through a NAT gateway. As traffic increases, the company's costs are increasing. The network engineer needs to change the connectivity to reduce the NAT gateway costs that result from the traffic between the EC2 instances and Amazon S3.

Which solution will meet these requirements?

A. Create a Direct Connect private VIF. Migrate the traffic from the public VIF to the private VIF.

B. Create an AWS Site-to-Site VPN tunnel over the existing public VIF.

C. Implement interface VPC endpoints for Amazon S3. Update the VPC route table.

D. Implement gateway VPC endpoints for Amazon S3. Update the VPC route table.

27) A company aims to enhance visibility into its AWS environment, which includes multiple VPCs connected to a transit gateway. This transit gateway links to an on-premises data center via an AWS Direct Connect gateway and two redundant Direct Connect connections utilizing transit VIFs. The company requires notifications each time a new route is advertised to AWS from on-premises over Direct Connect.

What should a network engineer do to meet these requirements?

A. Enable Amazon CloudWatch metrics on Direct Connect to monitor received routes. Configure a CloudWatch alarm to send notifications when routes change.

B. Onboard Transit Gateway Network Manager to Amazon CloudWatch Logs Insights. Use Amazon EventBridge (Amazon CloudWatch Events) to send notifications when routes change.

C. Set up an AWS Lambda function to periodically check the routes on the Direct Connect gateway and send notifications when routes change.

D. Enable Amazon CloudWatch Logs on the transit VIFs to monitor received routes. Create a metric filter and set an alarm on the filter to send notifications when routes change.

28) A software company provides a software-as-a-service (SaaS) accounting application hosted on the AWS Cloud. This application requires connectivity to the company's on-premises network. To handle the increasing demand for the application, the company has established two redundant 10 GB AWS Direct Connect connections between AWS and its on-premises network.

The company has existing encryption between its on-premises network and the colocation facility. Within the next few months, the company needs to encrypt traffic between AWS and the edge routers in the colocation facility, while maintaining its current bandwidth.

What should a network engineer do to meet these requirements with the LEAST operational overhead?

A. Deploy a new public VIF with encryption on the existing Direct Connect connections. Reroute traffic through the new public VIF.

B. Create a virtual private gateway. Deploy new AWS Site-to-Site VPN connections from on premises to the virtual private gateway. Reroute traffic from the Direct Connect private VIF to the new VPNs.

C. Deploy a new pair of 10 GB Direct Connect connections with MACsec. Configure MACsec on the edge routers. Reroute traffic to the new Direct Connect connections. Decommission the original Direct Connect connections.

D. Deploy a new pair of 10 GB Direct Connect connections with MACsec. Deploy a new public VIF on the new Direct Connect connections. Deploy two AWS Site-to-Site VPN connections on top of the new public VIF. Reroute traffic from the existing private VIF to the new Site-to-Site connections. Decommission the original Direct Connect connections.

29) A company hosts an application on Amazon EC2 instances behind an Application Load Balancer (ALB). Following a recent network security breach, a network engineer needs to collect and analyze logs that contain the client IP address, target IP address, target port, and user agent of each user accessing the application.

What is the MOST operationally efficient solution that meets these requirements?

A. Configure the ALB to store logs in an Amazon S3 bucket. Download the files from Amazon S3, and use a spreadsheet application to analyze the logs.

B. Configure the ALB to push logs to Amazon Kinesis Data Streams. Use Amazon Kinesis Data Analytics to analyze the logs.

C. Configure Amazon Kinesis Data Streams to stream data from the ALB to Amazon OpenSearch Service (Amazon Elasticsearch Service). Use search operations in Amazon OpenSearch Service (Amazon Elasticsearch Service) to analyze the data.

D. Configure the ALB to store logs in an Amazon S3 bucket. Use Amazon Athena to analyze the logs in Amazon S3.

30) A media company is launching a news website for a global audience. The website leverages Amazon CloudFront as its content delivery network. The backend is powered by Amazon EC2 Windows instances behind an Application Load Balancer (ALB). These instances are included in an Auto Scaling group. Customers access the website through service.example.com, which serves as the CloudFront custom domain name. The CloudFront origin is directed to an ALB using the domain name service-alb.example.com.

The company's security policy requires the traffic to be encrypted in transit at all times between the users and the backend.

Which combination of changes must the company make to meet this security requirement? (Choose three.)

A. Create a self-signed certificate for service.example.com. Import the certificate into AWS Certificate Manager (ACM). Configure CloudFront to use this imported SSL/TLS certificate. Change the default behavior to redirect HTTP to HTTPS.

B. Create a certificate for service.example.com by using AWS Certificate Manager (ACM). Configure CloudFront to use this custom SSL/TLS certificate. Change the default behavior to redirect HTTP to HTTPS.

C. Create a certificate with any domain name by using AWS Certificate Manager (ACM) for the EC2 instances. Configure the backend to use this certificate for its HTTPS listener. Specify the instance target type during the creation of a new target group that uses the HTTPS protocol for its targets. Attach the existing Auto Scaling group to this new target group.

D. Create a public certificate from a third-party certificate provider with any domain name for the EC2 instances.

Configure the backend to use this certificate for its HTTPS listener. Specify the instance target type during the creation of a new target group that uses the HTTPS protocol for its targets. Attach the existing Auto Scaling group to this new target group.

E. Create a certificate for service-alb.example.com by using AWS Certificate Manager (ACM). On the ALB add a new HTTPS listener that uses the new target group and the service-alb.example.com ACM certificate. Modify the CloudFront origin to use the HTTPS protocol only. Delete the HTTP listener on the ALB.

F. Create a self-signed certificate for service-alb.example.com. Import the certificate into AWS Certificate Manager (ACM). On the ALB add a new HTTPS listener that uses the new target group and the imported service-alb.example.com ACM certificate. Modify the CloudFront origin to use the HTTPS protocol only. Delete the HTTP listener on the ALB.

31) A company is running an application on Amazon EC2 instances behind a Network Load Balancer (NLB). To enhance the application's availability, a solutions architect has included EC2 instances in another Availability Zone. These instances have been added to the NLB target group.

The operations team of the company has observed that traffic is only being directed to the instances located in the initial Availability Zone.

What is the MOST operationally efficient solution to resolve this issue?

A. Enable the new Availability Zone on the NLB.

B. Create a new NLB for the instances in the second Availability Zone.

C. Enable proxy protocol on the NLB.

D. Create a new target group with the instances in both Availability Zones.

32) A network engineer is preparing to establish an Amazon EC2 Auto Scaling group to operate a Linux-based network appliance within a highly available architecture. As part of this setup, the engineer is configuring a new launch template for the Auto Scaling group.

The network appliance necessitates a secondary network interface, separate from the primary one. This interface will exclusively handle application traffic exchange with hosts over the internet. The company has established a Bring Your Own IP (BYOIP) pool, which includes an Elastic IP address designated for use as the public IP address for the second network interface.

How can the network engineer implement the required architecture?

A. In the launch template, configure the two network interfaces. Define the primary network interface to be created in one of the private subnets, and for the second network interface, select one of the public subnets. Choose the BYOIP pool ID as the source of public IP addresses.

B. Configure the primary network interface in a private subnet in the launch template. Utilize the user data option to execute a cloud-init script after boot to attach the second network interface from a subnet with auto-assign public IP addressing enabled.

C. Develop an AWS Lambda function to function as a lifecycle hook of the Auto Scaling group when an instance is launching. In the Lambda function, assign a network interface to an AWS Global Accelerator endpoint.

D. During creation of the Auto Scaling group, select subnets for the primary network interface. Use the user data option to run a cloud-init script to allocate a second network interface and to associate an Elastic IP address from the BYOIP pool.

33) A company delivers applications over the internet. An Amazon Route 53 public hosted zone serves as the authoritative DNS service for the company and its internet applications, all of which are offered under the same domain name.

A network engineer is working on a new version of one of these applications. All components of the application are hosted in the AWS Cloud. The application follows a three-tier architecture. The front end is delivered through Amazon EC2 instances deployed in public subnets, each assigned Elastic IP addresses. The backend components are deployed in private subnets using RFC1918 addresses.

The application's components must be able to access each other within the application's VPC using the same hostnames that are used over the public internet. The network engineer must also plan for future DNS changes, such as the addition of new hostnames or the removal of existing DNS entries. Which combination of steps will meet these requirements? (Choose three.)

A. Add a geoproximity routing policy in Route 53.

B. Create a Route 53 private hosted zone for the same domain name Associate the application's VPC with the new private hosted zone.

C. Enable DNS hostnames for the application's VPC.

D. Create entries in the private hosted zone for each name in the public hosted zone by using the corresponding private IP addresses.

E. Create an Amazon EventBridge (Amazon CloudWatch Events) rule that runs when AWS CloudTrail logs a Route 53 API call to the public hosted zone. Create an AWS Lambda function as the target of the rule. Configure the function to use the event information to update the private hosted zone.

F. Add the private IP addresses in the existing Route 53 public hosted zone.

34) A company is deploying an application using a series of containers in an Amazon Elastic Container Service (Amazon ECS) cluster. The company will utilize the Fargate launch type for its tasks. The containers will handle workloads that require SSL-initiated connectivity. Traffic must be able to flow to the application from other AWS accounts via private connectivity. The application must scale efficiently as the number of users increases.

Which solution will meet these requirements?

A. Select a Gateway Load Balancer (GLB) for the ECS service. Implement a lifecycle hook to add new tasks to the target group from Amazon ECS as needed for scaling. Include the GLB in the service definition. Establish a VPC peering connection for external AWS accounts and update the route tables to allow these accounts to access the GLB.

B. Select an Application Load Balancer (ALB) for the ECS service. Configure path-based routing rules to direct traffic to the containers registered in the target group. Include the ALB in the service definition. Create a VPC endpoint service for the ALB and share it with other AWS accounts.

C. Select an Application Load Balancer (ALB) for the ECS service. Configure path-based routing rules to direct traffic to the containers registered in the target group. Include the ALB in the service definition. Establish a VPC peering connection for external AWS accounts and update the route tables to allow these accounts to access the ALB.

D. Choose a Network Load Balancer (NLB) as the type of load balancer for the ECS service. Specify the NLB in the service definition. Create a VPC endpoint service for the NLB. Share the VPC endpoint service with other AWS accounts.

35) A company's development team has created a new product recommendation web service. This web service is hosted in a VPC with a CIDR block of 192.168.224.0/19. The company has deployed the web service on Amazon EC2 instances and configured an Auto Scaling group as the target for a Network Load Balancer (NLB).

The company aims to test whether users who receive product recommendations spend more money than those who do not. With a big sales event scheduled in 5 days, the company needs to integrate its existing production environment with the recommendation engine. The existing production environment is hosted in a VPC with a CIDR block of 192.168.128.0/17.

A network engineer must integrate the systems by designing a solution that results in the least possible disruption to the existing environments.

Which solution will meet these requirements?

A. Create a VPC peering connection between the web service VPC and the existing production VPC. Add a routing rule to the appropriate route table to allow data to flow to 192.168.224.0/19 from the existing production environment and to flow to 192.168.128.0/17 from the web service environment. Configure the relevant security groups and ACLs to allow the systems to communicate.

B. Ask the development team of the web service to redeploy the web service into the production VPC and integrate the systems there.

C. Create a VPC endpoint service. Associate the VPC endpoint service with the NLB for the web service. Create an interface VPC endpoint for the web service in the existing production VPC.

D. Create a transit gateway in the existing production environment. Create attachments to the production VPC and the web service VPC. Configure appropriate routing rules in the transit gateway and VPC route tables for 192.168.224.0/19 and 192.168.128.0/17. Configure the relevant security groups and ACLs to allow the systems to communicate.

36) A network engineer needs to update a company's hybrid network to support IPv6 for the upcoming release of a new application. The application is hosted in a VPC in the AWS Cloud. The company's current AWS infrastructure includes VPCs that are interconnected using a transit gateway. This transit gateway is linked to the on-premises network via AWS Direct Connect and AWS Site-to-Site VPN. The company's on-premises devices have been updated to meet the new IPv6 requirements.

To enable IPv6 for the existing VPC, the company has assigned a new IPv6 CIDR block to the VPC and configured the subnets for dual-stack support by assigning IPv6 addresses. New Amazon EC2 instances have been launched in these updated subnets to host the new application.

When updating the hybrid network to support IPv6, the network engineer must ensure that no changes are made to the existing infrastructure. Additionally, the engineer must block direct access to the instances' new IPv6 addresses from

the internet. However, outbound internet access from the instances must be allowed.

What is the MOST operationally efficient solution that meets these requirements?

A. Update the Direct Connect transit VIF and configure BGP peering with the AWS assigned IPv6 peering address. Create a new VPN connection that supports IPv6 connectivity. Add an egress-only internet gateway. Update any affected VPC security groups and route tables to provide connectivity within the VPC and between the VPC and the on-premises devices

B. Update the Direct Connect transit VIF and configure BGP peering with the AWS assigned IPv6 peering address. Update the existing VPN connection to support IPv6 connectivity. Add an egress-only internet gateway. Update any affected VPC security groups and route tables to provide connectivity within the VPC and between the VPC and the on-premises devices.

C. Create a Direct Connect transit VIF and configure BGP peering with the AWS assigned IPv6 peering address. Create a new VPN connection that supports IPv6 connectivity. Add an egress-only internet gateway. Update any affected VPC security groups and route tables to provide connectivity within the VPC and between the VPC and the on-premises devices.

D. Create a Direct Connect transit VIF and configure BGP peering with the AWS assigned IPv6 peering address. Create a new VPN connection that supports IPv6 connectivity. Add a NAT gateway. Update any affected VPC security groups and route tables to provide connectivity within the VPC and between the VPC and the on-premises devices.

37) A network engineer needs to enhance the security of encrypted data at Application Load Balancers (ALBs) by

implementing a unique random session key.

What should the network engineer do to meet this requirement?

A. Change the ALB security policy to a policy that supports TLS 1.2 protocol only

B. Use AWS Key Management Service (AWS KMS) to encrypt session keys

C. Associate an AWS WAF web ACL with the ALBs. and create a security rule to enforce forward secrecy (FS)

D. Change the ALB security policy to a policy that supports forward secrecy (FS)

38) A company has implemented a software-defined WAN (SD-WAN) solution to connect its offices. With a migration of workloads to AWS underway, the company needs to extend its SD-WAN to support connectivity to these new AWS-based workloads.

To achieve this, a network engineer intends to deploy AWS Transit Gateway Connect along with two SD-WAN virtual appliances. Company policy dictates that only one SD-WAN virtual appliance can process traffic from AWS workloads at any given time.

How should the network engineer configure routing to meet these requirements?

A. Add a static default route in the transit gateway route table to point to the secondary SD-WAN virtual appliance. Add routes that are more specific to point to the primary SD-WAN virtual appliance.

B. Configure the BGP community tag 7224:7300 on the primary SD-WAN virtual appliance for BGP routes toward the transit gateway.

C. Configure the AS_PATH prepend attribute on the secondary SD-WAN virtual appliance for BGP routes toward the transit gateway.

D. Disable equal-cost multi-path (ECMP) routing on the transit gateway for Transit Gateway Connect.

39) A company is preparing to deploy numerous software-defined WAN (SD-WAN) sites. The company is leveraging AWS Transit Gateway and has already deployed a transit gateway in the necessary AWS Region. A network engineer is tasked with deploying the SD-WAN hub virtual appliance within a VPC connected to the transit gateway. The solution should provide a minimum throughput of 5 Gbps from the SD-WAN hub virtual appliance to other VPCs attached to the transit gateway. Which solution will meet these requirements?

A. Create a new VPC for the SD-WAN hub virtual appliance. Establish two IPsec VPN connections between the SD-WAN hub virtual appliance and the transit gateway. Configure BGP over the IPsec VPN connections.

B. Assign a new CIDR block to the transit gateway. Create a new VPC for the SD-WAN hub virtual appliance. Attach the new VPC to the transit gateway with a VPC attachment. Add a transit gateway Connect attachment. Create a Connect peer and specify the GRE and BGP parameters. Create a route in the appropriate VPC for the SD-WAN hub virtual appliance to route to the transit gateway.

C. Set up a new VPC for the SD-WAN hub virtual appliance. Attach the new VPC to the transit gateway using a VPC attachment. Create two IPsec VPN connections between the SD-WAN hub virtual appliance and the transit gateway. Configure BGP over the IPsec VPN connections.

D. Allocate a new CIDR block to the transit gateway. Create a new VPC for the SD-WAN hub virtual appliance. Attach the new VPC to the transit gateway using a VPC attachment. Add a transit gateway Connect attachment. Establish a Connect peer and specify the VXLAN and BGP parameters. Create a route in the appropriate VPC for the SD-WAN hub virtual appliance to route to the transit gateway.

40) A company is implementing a new application on AWS that utilizes dynamic multicasting. The company has five VPCs, all connected to a transit gateway. Amazon EC2 instances within each VPC must be capable of dynamically registering to receive multicast transmissions.

How should a network engineer configure the AWS resources to meet these requirements?

A. Establish a static source multicast domain within the transit gateway. Associate the VPCs and relevant subnets with the multicast domain. Register the network interface of the multicast senders with the multicast domain. Modify the network ACLs to permit UDP traffic from the source to all receivers and UDP traffic sent to the multicast group address.

B. Establish a static source multicast domain within the transit gateway. Associate the VPCs and relevant subnets with the multicast domain. Register the network interface of the multicast senders with the multicast domain. Modify the network ACLs to permit TCP traffic from the source to all receivers and TCP traffic sent to the multicast group address.

C. Establish an Internet Group Management Protocol (IGMP)

multicast domain within the transit gateway. Associate the VPCs and relevant subnets with the multicast domain. Register the network interface of the multicast senders with the multicast domain. Modify the network ACLs to permit UDP traffic from the source to all receivers and UDP traffic sent to the multicast group address.

D. Establish an Internet Group Management Protocol (IGMP) multicast domain within the transit gateway. Associate the VPCs and relevant subnets with the multicast domain. Register the network interface of the multicast senders with the multicast domain. Modify the network ACLs to permit TCP traffic from the source to all receivers and TCP traffic sent to the multicast group address.

41) A company is developing new features for its e-commerce website, which will utilize multiple microservices accessed through various paths. These microservices will be hosted on Amazon Elastic Container Service (Amazon ECS). The company mandates the use of HTTPS for all its public websites and necessitates capturing the customer's source IP addresses.

A network engineer must implement a load balancing strategy that meets these requirements.
Which combination of actions should the network engineer take to accomplish this goal? (Choose two.)

A. Use a Network Load Balancer.

B. Retrieve client IP addresses by using the X-Forwarded-For header.

C. Use AWS App Mesh load balancing.

D. Retrieve client IP addresses by using the X-IP-Source header.

E. Use an Application Load Balancer.

42) A company is moving its containerized application to AWS. The architecture includes an ingress VPC with a Network Load Balancer (NLB) to route traffic to front-end pods in an Amazon Elastic Kubernetes Service (Amazon EKS) cluster. The front end will determine the user requesting access and send traffic to one of 10 services VPCs. Each service VPC will have an NLB to distribute traffic to the services pods in an EKS cluster.

The company is concerned about costs, as user traffic will generate more than 10 TB of data transfer from the ingress VPC to services VPCs per month. A network engineer needs to suggest a design for communication between the VPCs.

Which solution will meet these requirements at the LOWEST cost?

A. Create a transit gateway. Peer each VPC to the transit gateway. Use zonal DNS names for the NLB in the services VPCs to minimize cross-AZ traffic from the ingress VPC to the services VPCs.

B. Create an AWS PrivateLink endpoint in every Availability Zone in the ingress VPC. Each PrivateLink endpoint will point to the zonal DNS entry of the NLB in the services VPCs.

C. Create a VPC peering connection between the ingress VPC and each of the 10 services VPCs. Use zonal DNS names for the NLB in the services VPCs to minimize cross-AZ traffic from the ingress VPC to the services VPCs.

D. Create a transit gateway. Peer each VPC to the transit gateway. Turn off cross-AZ load balancing on the transit gateway. Use Regional DNS names for the NLB in the services VPCs.

43) A company has deployed stateful security appliances to multiple Availability Zones in a centralized shared services

VPC. The AWS environment includes a transit gateway that connects application VPCs to the shared services VPC. Workloads in the application VPCs are deployed in private subnets across multiple Availability Zones. The stateful appliances in the shared services VPC inspect all east-west (VPC-to-VPC) traffic.

Users have reported that inter-VPC traffic between different Availability Zones is dropping. A network engineer confirmed this issue by conducting ICMP pings between workloads in different Availability Zones across the application VPCs. The network engineer has eliminated security groups, stateful device configurations, and network ACLs as the potential causes of the dropped traffic.

What is causing the traffic to drop?

A. The stateful appliances and the transit gateway attachments are deployed in a separate subnet in the shared services VPC.

B. Appliance mode is not enabled on the transit gateway attachment to the shared services VPC.

C. The stateful appliances and the transit gateway attachments are deployed in the same subnet in the shared services VPC.

D. Appliance mode is not enabled on the transit gateway attachment to the application VPCs.

44) A company has numerous Amazon EC2 instances running in two production VPCs across all Availability Zones in the us-east-1 Region, named VPC A and VPC B.

A new security regulation mandates that all traffic between these production VPCs must be inspected before being routed to its final destination. To comply, the company deploys a new shared VPC containing a stateful firewall appliance and a transit gateway with a VPC attachment across all VPCs. This setup is intended to route traffic between VPC A and VPC B through the firewall appliance for inspection. However, during testing, the company observes that the transit gateway is dropping traffic when it moves between two Availability Zones.

What should a network engineer do to fix this issue with the LEAST management overhead?

A. In the shared VPC, replace the VPC attachment with a VPN attachment. Create a VPN tunnel between the transit gateway and the firewall appliance. Configure BGP.

B. Enable transit gateway appliance mode on the VPC attachment in VPC A and VPC B.

C. Enable transit gateway appliance mode on the VPC attachment in the shared VPC.

D. In the shared VPC, configure one VPC peering connection to VPC A and another VPC peering connection to VPC B.

45) The game's backend is hosted on Amazon EC2 instances within an Auto Scaling group. It utilizes the gRPC protocol for bidirectional streaming between game clients and the backend. To safeguard the game, the company requires filtering of incoming traffic based on the source IP address. Which solution will meet these requirements?

A. Configure an AWS Global Accelerator with an Application Load Balancer (ALB) endpoint. Attach the ALB to the Auto Scaling group. Configure an AWS WAF web ACL for the ALB to filter traffic based on the source IP address.

B. Configure an AWS Global Accelerator with a Network Load

Balancer (NLB) endpoint. Attach the NLB to the Auto Scaling group. Configure security groups for the EC2 instances to filter traffic based on the source IP address.

C. Configure an Amazon CloudFront distribution with an Application Load Balancer (ALB) endpoint. Attach the ALB to the Auto Scaling group. Configure an AWS WAF web ACL for the ALB to filter traffic based on the source IP address.

D. Configure an Amazon CloudFront distribution with a Network Load Balancer (NLB) endpoint. Attach the NLB to the Auto Scaling group. Configure security groups for the EC2 instances to filter traffic based on the source IP address.

46) A company has several VPCs in the us-east-1 Region. The company has launched a website within one of the VPCs. They aim to set up split-view DNS to enable internal access to the website from the VPCs and external access over the internet using the same domain name, example.com.

Which solution will meet these requirements?

A. Change the DHCP options for each VPC to use the IP address of an on-premises DNS server. Create a private hosted zone and a public hosted zone for example.com. Map the private hosted zone to the website's internal IP address. Map the public hosted zone to the website's external IP address.

B. Create Amazon Route 53 private hosted zones and public hosted zones that have the same name, example.com. Associate the VPCs with the private hosted zone. Create records in each hosted zone that determine how traffic is routed.

C. Create an Amazon Route 53 Resolver inbound endpoint for resolving example.com internally. Create a Route 53 public hosted zone for routing external DNS queries.

D. Create an Amazon Route 53 Resolver outbound endpoint for resolving example.com externally. Create a Route 53 private hosted zone for routing internal DNS queries.

47) A company has created a new web application hosted on Amazon EC2 instances that processes confidential data. The application requires scalability and must authenticate clients using certificates. It is designed to request a client's certificate and validate it during the initial handshake.

Which Elastic Load Balancing (ELB) solution will meet these requirements?

A. Configure an Application Load Balancer (ALB) that includes an HTTPS listener on port 443. Create an Auto Scaling group for the EC2 instances. Configure the Auto Scaling group as the target group of the ALB. Configure HTTPS as the protocol for the target group.

B. Configure a Network Load Balancer (NLB) that includes a TLS listener on port 443. Create an Auto Scaling group for the EC2 instances. Configure the Auto Scaling group as the target group of the NLB. Configure the NLB to terminate TLS. Configure TLS as the protocol for the target group.

C. Configure a Network Load Balancer (NLB) that includes a TCP listener on port 443. Create an Auto Scaling group for the EC2 instances. Configure the Auto Scaling group as the target group of the NLB. Configure TCP as the protocol for the target group.

D. Configure an Application Load Balancer (ALB) that includes a TLS listener on port 443. Create an Auto Scaling group for the EC2 instances. Configure the Auto Scaling group as the target group of the ALB. Configure TLS as the protocol for the target group.

48) A company is storing a large volume of shipping data in an on-premises data center. As part of a migration to AWS, a network engineer intends to use Amazon S3 to store this data in the initial phase. During this phase, an application located in the data center will need to privately access the data stored in an S3 bucket created by the company.

To facilitate this, the company has established an AWS Direct Connect connection with a private Virtual Interface (VIF) to link the on-premises data center to a VPC. The network engineer plans to leverage this Direct Connect connection for the hybrid cloud setup. The solution is required to be highly available.

What should the network engineer do next to implement this architecture?

A. Configure an S3 gateway endpoint in the VPC. Update VPC route tables to route traffic to the S3 gateway endpoint. Configure the S3 gateway endpoint DNS name in the on-premises application.

B. Configure an S3 interface endpoint in the VPC. Configure the S3 interface endpoint DNS name in the on-premises application.

C. Configure an S3 gateway endpoint in the VPC. Update VPC route tables to route traffic to the S3 gateway endpoint. Configure an HTTP proxy on an Amazon EC2 instance in the VPC to route traffic to the S3 gateway endpoint. Configure the HTTP proxy DNS name in the on-premises application.

D. Configure an S3 interface endpoint in the VPC. Update VPC route tables to route traffic to the S3 interface endpoint. Configure an HTTP proxy on an Amazon EC2 instance in the VPC to route traffic to the S3 interface endpoint. Configure the HTTP proxy DNS name in the on-premises application.

49) A company is architecting infrastructure on AWS, comprising three VPCs connected to a transit gateway: an application VPC, a backend VPC, and an inspection VPC. Compute instances in the application and backend VPCs are deployed across Availability Zone A and Availability Zone B. Stateful firewalls, acting as layer 7 virtual firewall appliances, are deployed in the same Availability Zones within the inspection VPC, which serves as a shared services VPC. All traffic must pass through the inspection VPC's stateful firewalls to comply with a security policy requiring traffic inspection. IP addresses across the three VPCs do not overlap. The network engineer must ensure that traffic between the application and backend VPCs is routed through the inspection VPC's stateful firewalls. Which solution will meet these requirements?

A. Create IPsec VPN connections between the transit gateway and the virtual firewall appliances.

B. Configure Virtual Router Redundancy Protocol (VRRP) on the virtual firewall appliances.

C. Set up BGP between the transit gateway and the virtual firewall appliances.

D. Enable transit gateway appliance mode for the VPC attachment to the inspection VPC.

50) A company is using Amazon Route 53 to host a public hosted zone and wishes to configure DNS Security Extensions (DNSSEC) signing for it. The company's critical applications are hosted in the us-west-2 Region.

To enable DNSSEC, the company created a symmetric, customer-managed key in the us-west-2 Region using AWS Key Management Service (AWS KMS). However, the network engineer discovers that this existing AWS KMS key cannot be used to create a key-signing key (KSK). How can the network engineer resolve this issue?

A. Recreate a symmetric, customer managed, multi-Region key in the us-east-1 Region. Use this key to create a KSK.

B. Recreate a symmetric, customer managed, single-Region key in us-west-2. Use this key to create a KSK.

C. Recreate an asymmetric, customer managed key with an ECC_NIST_P256 key spec in the us-east-1 Region. Use this key to create a KSK.

D. Recreate an asymmetric, customer managed key with an ECC_NIST_P256 key spec in us-west-2. Use this key to create a KSK.

51) A company is migrating multiple applications from two on-premises data centers to AWS, spreading the applications across two AWS Regions: us-east-1 and us-west-2. The network team is establishing connectivity to the AWS environment, setting up AWS Direct Connect connections at two locations.

Direct Connect connection 1 connects to the first data center in us-east-1, while Direct Connect connection 2 connects to the second data center in us-west-2. Both Direct Connect connections are linked to a single Direct Connect gateway using transit VIFs. The Direct Connect gateway is associated with transit gateways deployed in each Region. All traffic to and from AWS must pass through the first data center, with the second data center taking over traffic in case of failure.

How should the network team configure BGP to meet these requirements?

A. Configure the local preference BGP community tag 7224:7300 for the transit VIF connected to Direct Connect connection 1.

B. Configure the local preference BGP community tag 7224:9300 for the transit VIF connected to Direct Connect connection 2.

C. Use the AS_PATH attribute to prepend the additional hop for the transit VIF connected to Direct Connect connection 2.

D. Use the AS_PATH attribute to prepend the additional hop for the transit VIF connected to Direct Connect connection 1.

52) An ecommerce company operates a business-critical application on Amazon EC2 instances within a VPC. The development team has been conducting tests on new versions of the application using test EC2 instances. They now wish to subject the new application version to production traffic for testing purposes, aiming to identify and resolve any potential issues before deploying the new version to all servers. Which solution will meet this requirement with no impact on the end user's experience?

A. Configure Amazon Route 53 weighted routing policies by configuring records that have the same name and type as each of the instances. Assign relative weights to the production instances and the test instances.

B. Create an Application Load Balancer with weighted target groups. Add more than one target group to the forward action of a listener rule. Specify a weight for each target group.

C. Implement Traffic Mirroring to replay the production requests to the test instances. Configure the source as the production instances. Configure the target as the test instances.

D. Configure a NGINX proxy in front of the production servers.

Use the NGINX mirroring capability.

53) A company is hosting its ecommerce application on Amazon EC2 instances behind an Application Load Balancer. The EC2 instances reside in a private subnet using the default DHCP options. Internet connectivity is provided through a NAT gateway configured in the public subnet.

During a third-party security audit, a DNS exfiltration vulnerability is identified in the company's infrastructure. To address this vulnerability, the company needs to implement a highly available solution.

Which solution will meet these requirements MOST cost-effectively?

A. Configure a BIND server with DNS filtering. Modify the DNS servers in the DHCP options set.

B. Use Amazon Route 53 Resolver DNS Firewall. Configure a domain list with a rule group.

C. Use AWS Network Firewall with domain name filtering.

D. Configure an Amazon Route 53 Resolver outbound endpoint with rules to filter and block suspicious traffic.

54) A company is utilizing Amazon Route 53 Resolver for its hybrid DNS infrastructure. The company is leveraging Route 53 Resolver forwarding rules to handle authoritative domains hosted on on-premises DNS servers. Hybrid network connectivity is established using an AWS Site-to-Site VPN connection.

A new governance policy mandates logging for DNS traffic originating in the AWS Cloud. The policy also requires the company to query DNS traffic to ascertain the source IP

address of the resources from which the query originated, along with the requested DNS name.

Which solution will meet these requirements?

A. Create VPC flow logs for all VPCs. Send the logs to Amazon CloudWatch Logs. Use CloudWatch Logs Insights to query the IP address and DNS name.

B. Configure Route 53 Resolver query logging for all VPCs. Send the logs to Amazon CloudWatch Logs. Use CloudWatch Logs Insights to query the IP address and DNS name.

C. Configure DNS logging for the Site-to-Site VPN connection. Send the logs to an Amazon S3 bucket. Use Amazon Athena to query the IP address and DNS name.

D. Modify the existing Route 53 Resolver rules to configure logging. Send the logs to an Amazon S3 bucket. Use Amazon Athena to query the IP address and DNS name.

55) A company has deployed a web application on AWS, utilizing an Application Load Balancer (ALB) across multiple Availability Zones. The ALB directs traffic to AWS Lambda functions. The web application also utilizes Amazon CloudWatch metrics for monitoring. Users have reported issues with certain parts of the web application not loading correctly. To troubleshoot the problem, a network engineer has enabled access logging for the ALB. What should the network engineer do next to determine which errors the ALB is receiving?

A. Send the logs to Amazon CloudWatch Logs. Review the ALB logs in CloudWatch Insights to determine which error messages the ALB is receiving.

B. Configure the Amazon S3 bucket destination. Use Amazon Athena to determine which error messages the ALB is receiving.

C. Configure the Amazon S3 bucket destination. After Amazon CloudWatch Logs pulls the ALB logs from the S3 bucket automatically, review the logs in CloudWatch Logs to determine which error messages the ALB is receiving.

D. Send the logs to Amazon CloudWatch Logs. Use the Amazon Athena CloudWatch Connector to determine which error messages the ALB is receiving.

56) A real estate company is developing an internal application for real estate agents to upload photos and videos of properties. The application will store these media files as objects in an Amazon S3 bucket and use Amazon DynamoDB to store corresponding metadata. The S3 bucket will be configured to trigger an Amazon Simple Queue Service (Amazon SQS) queue with PUT events for new object uploads.

A compute cluster of Amazon EC2 instances will poll the SQS queue to identify newly uploaded objects. The cluster will retrieve these objects, perform proprietary image and video recognition and classification, update metadata in DynamoDB, and replace the objects with new watermarked versions. The company prefers not to use public IP addresses for the EC2 instances.

Which networking design solution will meet these requirements MOST cost-effectively as application usage increases?

A. Place the EC2 instances in a public subnet. Disable the Auto-assign Public IP option while launching the EC2 instances. Create an internet gateway. Attach the internet gateway to the VPC. In the public subnet's route table, add a default route that points to the internet gateway.

B. Place the EC2 instances in a private subnet. Create a NAT gateway in a public subnet in the same Availability Zone. Create an internet gateway. Attach the internet gateway to the VPC. In the public subnet's route table, add a default route that points to the internet gateway

C. Place the EC2 instances in a private subnet. Create an interface VPC endpoint for Amazon SQS. Create gateway VPC endpoints for Amazon S3 and DynamoDB.

D. Place the EC2 instances in a private subnet. Create a gateway VPC endpoint for Amazon SQS. Create interface VPC endpoints for Amazon S3 and DynamoDB.

57) A company's network engineer is architecting a hybrid DNS solution for an AWS Cloud workload. Various teams wish to oversee the DNS hostnames for their applications within their development environment. The solution must seamlessly integrate these application-specific hostnames with the centrally managed DNS hostnames from the on-premises network and ensure bidirectional name resolution. Additionally, the solution should minimize management overhead.

Which combination of steps should the network engineer take to meet these requirements? (Choose three.)

A. Use an Amazon Route 53 Resolver inbound endpoint.

B. Modify the DHCP options set by setting a custom DNS server value.

C. Use an Amazon Route 53 Resolver outbound endpoint.

D. Create DNS proxy servers.

E. Create Amazon Route 53 private hosted zones.

F. Set up a zone transfer between Amazon Route 53 and the on-premises DNS.

58) A company has deployed an application in a VPC that uses a NAT gateway for outbound internet traffic. A network engineer observes a significant amount of suspicious network traffic from the VPC to IP addresses on a deny list. The engineer needs to identify the AWS resources responsible for this traffic while minimizing costs and administrative overhead.

Which solution will meet these requirements?

A. Launch an Amazon EC2 instance in the VPC. Use Traffic Mirroring by specifying the NAT gateway as the source and the EC2 instance as the destination. Analyze the captured traffic by using open-source tools to identify the AWS resources that are generating the suspicious traffic.

B. Use VPC flow logs. Launch a security information and event management (SIEM) solution in the VPC. Configure the SIEM solution to ingest the VPC flow logs. Run queries on the SIEM solution to identify the AWS resources that are generating the suspicious traffic.

C. Use VPC flow logs. Publish the flow logs to a log group in Amazon CloudWatch Logs. Use CloudWatch Logs Insights to query the flow logs to identify the AWS resources that are generating the suspicious traffic.

D. Configure the VPC to stream the network traffic directly to an Amazon Kinesis data stream. Send the data from the Kinesis data stream to an Amazon Kinesis Data Firehose delivery stream to store the data in Amazon S3. Use Amazon Athena to query the data to identify the AWS resources that are generating the suspicious traffic.

59) A company is deploying a non-web application using an AWS load balancer. The targets for this load balancer are on-premises servers accessible via AWS Direct Connect. The company needs to ensure that the source IP addresses of clients connecting to the application are preserved and passed through to the end servers.

How can this requirement be achieved?

A. Use a Network Load Balancer to automatically preserve the source IP address.

B. Use a Network Load Balancer and enable the X-Forwarded-For attribute.

C. Use a Network Load Balancer and enable the ProxyProtocol v2 attribute.

D. Use an Application Load Balancer to automatically preserve the source IP address in the X-Forwarded-For header.

60) A company is deploying a new stateless web application on AWS. The application will run on Amazon EC2 instances located in private subnets behind an Application Load Balancer (ALB). These EC2 instances are part of an Auto Scaling group. Additionally, the company has a stateful management application for administration purposes, which will also run on EC2 instances in a separate Auto Scaling group.

The company wants to access the management application using the same URL as the web application, but with a "/ management" path prefix. The protocol, hostname, and port number must remain consistent for both applications. Access to the management application needs to be restricted to the company's on-premises IP address space. An SSL/TLS certificate from AWS Certificate Manager (ACM) will secure the

web application.

Which combination of steps should a network engineer take to meet these requirements? (Choose two.)

A. Insert a rule for the load balancer HTTPS listener. Configure the rule to check the path-pattern condition type for the / management prefix and to check the source-ip condition type for the on-premises IP address space. Forward requests to the management application target group if there is a match. Edit the management application target group and enable stickiness.

B. Modify the default rule for the load balancer HTTPS listener. Configure the rule to check the path-pattern condition type for the /management prefix and to check the source-ip condition type for the on-premises IP address space. Forward requests to the management application target group if there is not a match. Enable group-level stickiness in the rule attributes.

C. Insert a rule for the load balancer HTTPS listener. Configure the rule to check the path-pattern condition type for the / management prefix and to check the X-Forwarded-For HTTP header for the on-premises IP address space. Forward requests to the management application target group if there is a match. Enable group-level stickiness in the rule attributes.

D. Modify the default rule for the load balancer HTTPS listener. Configure the rule to check the path-pattern condition type for the /management prefix and to check the source-ip condition type for the on-premises IP address space. Forward requests to the web application target group if there is not a match.

E. Forward all requests to the web application target group. Edit the web application target group and disable stickiness.

61) A security team is conducting an audit of a company's AWS deployment. They are concerned that two applications might

be accessing resources that should be restricted by network ACLs and security groups. These applications are deployed across two Amazon Elastic Kubernetes Service (Amazon EKS) clusters, using the Amazon VPC Container Network Interface (CNI) plugin for Kubernetes. The clusters reside in separate subnets within the same VPC and are configured with a Cluster Autoscaler.

The security team needs to identify which POD IP addresses are communicating with which services throughout the VPC. They aim to minimize the number of flow logs and focus on traffic from only the two applications.

Which solution will meet these requirements with the LEAST operational overhead?

A. Create VPC flow logs in the default format. Create a filter to gather flow logs only from the EKS nodes. Include the srcaddr field and the dstaddr field in the flow logs.

B. Create VPC flow logs in a custom format. Set the EKS nodes as the resource Include the pkt-srcaddr field and the pkt-dstaddr field in the flow logs.

C. Create VPC flow logs in a custom format. Set the application subnets as resources. Include the pkt-srcaddr field and the pkt-dstaddr field in the flow logs.

D. Create VPC flow logs in a custom format. Create a filter to gather flow logs only from the EKS nodes. Include the pkt-srcaddr field and the pkt-dstaddr field in the flow logs.

62) An IoT company sells hardware sensor modules that periodically transmit temperature, humidity, pressure, and location data using the MQTT messaging protocol. These modules send data to the company's on-premises MQTT brokers, which operate on Linux servers behind a load

balancer. The sensor modules have hardcoded public IP addresses for broker communication.

As the company expands and gains global customers, the existing solution struggles to scale and introduces latency due to the company's worldwide presence. Consequently, the company decides to migrate its entire infrastructure to the AWS Cloud without reconfiguring the already deployed sensor modules. The solution must also minimize latency.

The company migrates the MQTT brokers to Amazon EC2 instances.

What should the company do next to meet these requirements?

A. Place the EC2 instances behind a Network Load Balancer (NLB). Configure TCP listeners. Use Bring Your Own IP (BYOIP) from the on-premises network with the NLB.

B. Place the EC2 instances behind a Network Load Balancer (NLB). Configure TCP listeners. Create an AWS Global Accelerator in front of the NLUse Bring Your Own IP (BYOIP) from the on-premises network with Global Accelerator.

C. Place the EC2 instances behind an Application Load Balancer (ALB). Configure TCP listeners. Create an AWS Global Accelerator in front of the ALB. Use Bring Your Own IP (BYOIP) from the on-premises network with Global Accelerator

D. Place the EC2 instances behind an Amazon CloudFront distribution. Use Bring Your Own IP (BYOIP) from the on-premises network with CloudFront.

63) The company utilizes AWS Direct Connect to link its corporate network to numerous VPCs within the same AWS account and Region. Each VPC is assigned its private VIF and

virtual LAN on the Direct Connect connection. As the company expands, it is approaching the limit for VPCs and private VIFs per connection.

What is the MOST scalable way to add VPCs with on-premises connectivity?

A. Provision a new Direct Connect connection to handle the additional VPCs. Use the new connection to connect additional VPCs.

B. Create virtual private gateways for each VPC that is over the service quota. Use AWS Site-to-Site VPN to connect the virtual private gateways to the corporate network.

C. Create a Direct Connect gateway, and add virtual private gateway associations to the VPCs. Configure a private VIF to connect to the corporate network.

D. Create a transit gateway, and attach the VPCs. Create a Direct Connect gateway, and associate it with the transit gateway. Create a transit VIF to the Direct Connect gateway.

64) A network engineer has launched an Amazon EC2 instance in a private subnet within a VPC that lacks a public subnet. This EC2 instance is responsible for hosting application code that transmits messages to an Amazon Simple Queue Service (Amazon SQS) queue. The subnet is configured with the default network ACL and has not been altered. Additionally, the EC2 instance is using the default security group without any modifications.

Despite these configurations, the SQS queue is not receiving messages.

Which of the following are possible causes of this problem? (Choose two.)

A. The EC2 instance is not attached to an IAM role that allows write operations to Amazon SQS.

B. The security group is blocking traffic to the IP address range used by Amazon SQS.

C. There is no interface VPC endpoint configured for Amazon SQS.

D. The network ACL is blocking return traffic from Amazon SQS.

E. There is no route configured in the subnet route table for the IP address range used by Amazon SQS.

65) Your organization has recently set up a 1-Gbps AWS Direct Connect connection. After ordering the cross-connect from the Direct Connect location provider to the port on your router in the same facility, the router needs to be configured correctly to enable the use of your first virtual interface.

What are the minimum requirements for your router?

A. 1-Gbps Multi Mode Fiber Interface, 802.1Q VLAN, Peer IP Address, BGP Session with MD5.

B. 1-Gbps Single Mode Fiber Interface, 802.1Q VLAN, Peer IP Address, BGP Session with MD5.

C. IPsec Parameters, Pre-Shared key, Peer IP Address, BGP Session with MD5.

D. BGP Session with MD5, 802.1Q VLAN, Route-Map, Prefix List, IPsec encrypted GRE Tunnel.

ANSWERS AND EXPLANATION

1) A is correct.

Explanation:

To meet the requirements of encryption in transit and mutual TLS for two-way authentication between the client and the backend while using gRPC over TCP port 443, the most suitable solution is to use a Network Load Balancer (NLB) with a TCP listener. The NLB can handle a large number of simultaneous connections and ensure that traffic remains encrypted end-to-end without decryption between the client and the backend.

Here's why the other options are not ideal:

B. Install the AWS Load Balancer Controller for Kubernetes. Configure an Application Load Balancer with an HTTPS listener on port 443 using the controller to forward traffic to the backend service Pods' IP addresses.

An Application Load Balancer (ALB) with an HTTPS listener would require the load balancer to handle TLS termination, meaning the traffic would be decrypted at the ALB and then re-encrypted when sent to the backend. This does not meet the requirement of keeping the data encrypted end-to-end.

C. Create a target group and add the EKS managed node group's Auto Scaling group as a target. Create an Application Load

Balancer with an HTTPS listener on port 443 to forward traffic to the target group.

Similar to option B, using an ALB with an HTTPS listener involves TLS termination at the load balancer, which does not fulfill the requirement for end-to-end encryption without decryption in transit.

D. Create a target group and add the EKS managed node group's Auto Scaling group as a target. Create a Network Load Balancer with a TLS listener on port 443 to forward traffic to the target group.

While a Network Load Balancer with a TLS listener can be configured, it's more common to use a TCP listener for gRPC traffic to ensure that encryption is handled end-to-end by the application. The TLS listener might involve additional complexity and is not necessary for meeting the requirements.

Therefore, the best solution is:

A. Install the AWS Load Balancer Controller for Kubernetes. Using that controller, configure a Network Load Balancer with a TCP listener on port 443 to forward traffic to the IP addresses of the backend service Pods.

ALB does support HTTP/2 and gRPC workloads. However, the title mentions that the company needs to use mutual TLS for mutual authentication between the client and the backend. This means that traffic cannot be decrypted between the client and the service backend. Since the ALB will terminate the TLS connection and decrypt the traffic, it does not meet the requirements in the title.

In contrast, NLB can forward TCP traffic without decrypting the traffic, so it is more suitable for meeting the needs described in the title.

Reference:

https://docs.aws.amazon.com/prescriptive-guidance/latest/
patterns/configure-mutual-tls-authentication-for-applications-
running-on-amazon-eks.html

2) A is correct.

Explanation:

To meet the requirements of a highly available web server
positioned behind an Elastic Load Balancer with HTTPS traffic,
TLS offloading, and the capability to capture the user's IP address
for accurate logging, the best solution is to use an Application
Load Balancer (ALB) with path-based routing rules. The ALB
supports HTTPS listeners and can include the X-Forwarded-For
header, which provides the client's IP address to the backend
servers.

Here's why the other options are not ideal:

B. Deploy an Application Load Balancer with an HTTPS listener
for each domain. Implement host-based routing rules to direct
traffic to the appropriate target group for each domain. Ensure
the X-Forwarded-For request header is included with traffic sent
to the targets.

Deploying an ALB for each domain is unnecessary and increases
complexity and cost. A single ALB with path-based routing can
handle requests based on the URL efficiently.

C. Deploy a Network Load Balancer with a TLS listener.
Implement path-based routing rules to direct traffic to
the appropriate target group. Configure client IP address

preservation for traffic sent to the targets.

Network Load Balancers (NLBs) are typically used for high-performance, low-latency Layer 4 traffic. They do not support path-based routing and are less suitable for HTTPS termination and routing based on URL paths compared to ALBs.

D. Deploy a Network Load Balancer with a TLS listener for each domain. Implement host-based routing rules to direct traffic to the appropriate target group for each domain. Configure client IP address preservation for traffic sent to the targets.

Similar to option C, using an NLB is less suitable for this scenario due to the lack of path-based routing support and the complexity of managing multiple NLBs.

Therefore, the best solution is:

A. Deploy an Application Load Balancer with an HTTPS listener. Implement path-based routing rules to direct traffic to the appropriate target group. Ensure the X-Forwarded-For request header is included with traffic sent to the targets.

3) A is correct:

A. Configure the ALB in a private subnet of the VPC. Attach an internet gateway without adding routes in the subnet route tables to point to the internet gateway. Configure the accelerator with endpoint groups that include the ALB endpoint. Configure the ALB's security group to only allow inbound traffic from the internet on the ALB listener port.

Placing the ALB in a private subnet ensures it is not directly accessible from the internet.

Attaching an internet gateway without adding routes in the subnet route tables prevents internet access to the ALB, ensuring that traffic is routed through the AWS Global Accelerator.

Configuring the accelerator with endpoint groups that include the ALB endpoint ensures that traffic is directed through the Global Accelerator.

Setting the ALB's security group to only allow inbound traffic from the internet on the ALB listener port ensures that the ALB only accepts traffic from the AWS Global Accelerator, preventing direct access from the internet.

This setup effectively meets the requirements of the scenario by ensuring that the application is only accessible through the AWS Global Accelerator and not directly over the internet to the ALB endpoint.

Reference:

This is not a normal scenario of attaching IGW to EC2 instance by creating a route in subnet.

Please read the below link typically describing ELB integration with AWS Global accelerator (and the last line of the extract)

https://docs.aws.amazon.com/global-accelerator/latest/dg/secure-vpc-connections.html

"When you add an internal Application Load Balancer or an Amazon EC2 instance endpoint in AWS Global Accelerator, you enable internet traffic to flow directly to and from the endpoint in Virtual Private Clouds (VPCs) by targeting it in a private subnet. The VPC that contains the load balancer or EC2 instance must have an internet gateway attached to it, to indicate that the VPC accepts internet traffic. However, you don't need public IP addresses on the load balancer or EC2 instance. You also don't need an associated internet gateway route for the subnet."

4) Correct answer: C. Create VPC endpoint services powered by

AWS PrivateLink in the central shared services VPC. Create VPC endpoints in each application VPC.

Explanation:

VPC endpoints with AWS PrivateLink provide private connectivity between VPCs and AWS services without exposing the traffic to the public internet. This ensures a high level of security for data exchange between the application VPCs and the central shared services VPC.

Using VPC endpoints also simplifies the network architecture and reduces the attack surface compared to other options like VPNs or transit gateways.

Additionally, AWS PrivateLink scales automatically to handle increased traffic and can accommodate future business units accessing data from the central shared services VPC.

Options A, B, and D involve creating complex network architectures with potentially more exposure to security risks and may not provide the same level of scalability and simplicity as using AWS PrivateLink for VPC endpoints.

5) Correct answer: A

A. Review the Amazon CloudWatch metrics for VirtualInterfaceBpsEgress and VirtualInterfaceBpsIngress to determine which VIF is sending the highest throughput during the period in which slowness is observed. Create a new 10 Gbps dedicated connection. Shift traffic from the existing dedicated connection to the new dedicated connection.

Explanation:

By reviewing the CloudWatch metrics for VirtualInterfaceBpsEgress and VirtualInterfaceBpsIngress, the network engineer can identify the VIF responsible for the spikes in throughput.

Creating a new 10 Gbps dedicated connection will provide additional bandwidth to accommodate the increased traffic during peak periods.

Shifting traffic from the existing connection to the new one will help alleviate the congestion on the current connection and improve performance for all VPCs.

Option A is the most appropriate solution as it addresses the identified issue of periodic spikes in throughput and provides a scalable solution for future growth.

Reference:

https://docs.aws.amazon.com/directconnect/latest/UserGuide/dedicated_connection.html

> "You cannot change the port speed after you create the connection request. To change the port speed, you must create and configure a new connection."

6) Correct answer: AB

Option A, deploying the SaaS service endpoint behind a Network Load Balancer (NLB), allows the provider to present a single IP address to customers, while maintaining a highly available and scalable architecture. This is achieved by mapping the NLB's IP address to the SaaS service endpoint.

Option B, configuring an endpoint service, enables customers to connect to the SaaS service endpoint using their own private IP addresses. This allows customers to avoid IP address overlap with the provider's AWS deployment and provides a secure, private connection to the SaaS service without traversing the internet.

Reference:

https://docs.aws.amazon.com/vpc/latest/privatelink/
privatelink-access-saas.html

7) The network engineer should implement a combination of three steps to meet all the workload requirements for the healthcare company:

D. Use AWS Direct Connect with MACsec support for connectivity to the cloud.

E. Use Gateway Load Balancers to insert third-party firewalls for inline traffic inspection.

F. Configure AWS Shield Advanced and ensure that it is configured on all public assets.

Here's why these options address the specific needs:

D. AWS Direct Connect with MACsec: This provides a secure and dedicated connection between the on-premises environment and the AWS cloud. MACsec encrypts data in transit, fulfilling the requirement for encrypted communication.

E. Gateway Load Balancers with Third-Party Firewalls: Gateway Load Balancers (GLBs) can be configured to integrate with third-party firewalls. This allows for inline traffic inspection within the cloud before traffic exits to the on-premises environment or the internet, ensuring compliance with the security inspection mandate.

F. AWS Shield Advanced: This managed service offers advanced DDoS protection with automatic mitigation techniques and cost protection against scaling charges during an attack. It's crucial to configure Shield Advanced on all internet-facing public assets (components accessible to patients) to defend against DDoS attacks and potentially mitigate financial liability for DDoS-related resource scaling.

Let's analyze why the other options are not part of the ideal solution:

A. Traffic Mirroring: While it can capture traffic copies for analysis, it doesn't directly address encryption or traffic inspection requirements.

B. AWS WAF: This web application firewall is excellent for protecting web applications against common attacks, but it wouldn't provide the level of traffic inspection needed for all traffic exiting the cloud environment.

C. AWS Lambda with Deny Rules: Automated blocking based on IP addresses can be helpful, but it's a reactive approach and might not be efficient for comprehensive DDoS mitigation.

By implementing a combination of secure connectivity, inline traffic inspection, and advanced DDoS protection, the network engineer can achieve a robust and secure architecture for the healthcare company's workload migration to the AWS Cloud.

References:

D

https://docs.aws.amazon.com/directconnect/latest/UserGuide/MACsec.html

E

https://docs.aws.amazon.com/elasticloadbalancing/latest/gateway/introduction.html

F

https://docs.aws.amazon.com/waf/latest/developerguide/ddos-advanced-summary.html

8) The two most suitable options for the network engineer to investigate the NAT gateway traffic surge are:

A. Enable VPC flow logs on the NAT gateway's elastic network interface. Publish the logs to a log group in Amazon CloudWatch Logs. Use CloudWatch Logs Insights to query and analyze the logs.

D. Enable VPC flow logs on the NAT gateway's elastic network interface. Publish the logs to an Amazon S3 bucket. Create a custom table for the S3 bucket in Amazon Athena to query and analyze the logs.

Here's why these options are effective:

VPC Flow Logs: Enabling VPC flow logs on the NAT gateway's interface captures detailed information about the network traffic flowing through the gateway. This data includes source and destination IP addresses, ports, bytes transferred, etc.

Analysis with CloudWatch Logs or Athena: Both CloudWatch Logs Insights and Athena allow the engineer to analyze the captured flow logs. CloudWatch Logs Insights provides a user-friendly interface for querying and filtering logs, while Athena offers a powerful SQL-like query language for in-depth analysis.

Let's see why the other options are not ideal solutions:

B. NAT Gateway Access Logs (Non-existent): AWS doesn't offer dedicated access logs for NAT gateways. Option A leverages VPC flow logs, which provide the necessary traffic information.

C. Traffic Mirroring (Resource Intensive): While mirroring traffic to another EC2 instance allows analysis with tools like tcpdump or Wireshark, it can be resource-intensive and less scalable compared to log-based analysis.

E. S3 with Limited Functionality for Access Logs (Redundant with D): Option D already covers publishing flow logs to S3 and analyzing them with Athena. Option E focuses on non-existent NAT gateway access logs, making it irrelevant.

Therefore, enabling VPC flow logs and analyzing them using either CloudWatch Logs Insights or Athena provides a comprehensive and efficient approach for the network engineer to investigate the cause of the increased NAT gateway usage.

Reference:

https://aws.amazon.com/premiumsupport/knowledge-center/vpc-find-traffic-sources-nat-gateway/

9) Correct answer: C. Create an egress-only Internet gateway in the VPC. Add a route to the existing subnet route tables to point IPv6 traffic to the egress-only internet gateway.

Explanation:

Since the company's policy prohibits IPv6 traffic from the public internet and mandates that the company's servers initiate all IPv6 connectivity, an egress-only internet gateway is the appropriate solution. An egress-only internet gateway allows IPv6-connected instances in the private subnet to initiate outbound IPv6 traffic to the internet, but prevents inbound traffic from reaching those instances.

A. Creating an internet gateway and a NAT gateway in the VPC with a route pointing IPv6 traffic to the NAT gateway would allow outbound IPv6 traffic, but it would also potentially allow inbound traffic, which goes against the company's policy.

B. Creating an internet gateway and a NAT instance in the VPC with a route pointing IPv6 traffic to the NAT instance would have similar issues as option A, potentially allowing inbound traffic.

D. Creating an egress-only internet gateway in the VPC and configuring a security group that denies all inbound traffic, then associating the security group with the egress-only internet gateway, is not a standard method for restricting inbound IPv6 traffic. The egress-only internet gateway itself is designed to handle outbound IPv6 traffic, while security groups primarily manage inbound traffic.

Reference:

https://docs.aws.amazon.com/vpc/latest/userguide/egress-only-internet-gateway.html

- An egress-only internet gateway is a horizontally scaled, redundant, and highly available VPC component that allows outbound communication over IPv6 from instances in your VPC to the internet, and prevents the internet from initiating an IPv6 connection with your instances.

- An egress-only internet gateway is for use with IPv6 traffic only. To enable outbound-only internet communication over IPv4, use a NAT gateway instead.

10) The best solution to deliver Network Firewall flow logs quickly to the Amazon OpenSearch Service cluster is:

B. Create an Amazon Kinesis Data Firehose delivery stream that includes the Amazon OpenSearch Service (Amazon Elasticsearch Service) cluster as the destination. Configure flow logs for the firewall and set the Kinesis Data Firehose delivery stream as the destination for the Network Firewall flow logs.

Here's why this option is ideal for fast log delivery:

Kinesis Data Firehose: This service is specifically designed for streaming large data volumes like logs from sources like Network Firewall to various destinations, including Amazon OpenSearch Service. It offers buffer capabilities and batching to optimize data delivery.

Let's explore why the other options are less suitable:

A. S3 Bucket and Lambda Function: While S3 can store logs, it introduces an extra step with the Lambda function for processing and loading them into OpenSearch. This adds latency compared to the direct streaming approach of Kinesis Data Firehose.

C. Direct Destination to OpenSearch: While technically possible, Network Firewall logs can be voluminous. OpenSearch might not be optimized for real-time ingestion of such high-velocity data streams, potentially causing delays or performance issues.

D. Kinesis Data Stream (Deprecated): Amazon Kinesis Data Streams is an older service superseded by Kinesis Data Firehose. Data Firehose offers additional features like data transformation and conversion, making it a better fit for log delivery scenarios.

Therefore, using Kinesis Data Firehose as a delivery stream provides a more efficient and scalable solution for streaming Network Firewall logs to the Amazon OpenSearch Service cluster.

Reference:

https://aws.amazon.com/blogs/networking-and-content-delivery/how-to-analyze-aws-network-firewall-logs-using-amazon-opensearch-service-part-1/

11) Options B and D are the correct choices to enable all development teams to mount EFS file systems.

Both options leverage the power of Route 53 Resolver to ensure proper DNS resolution for EFS mount target addresses.

B. Route 53 Resolver with AmazonProvidedDNS: This approach provides a centralized solution, eliminating the need for individual configuration changes on each BIND server.

D. Route 53 Resolver Rule (While not the most efficient for EFS specifically): This option offers flexibility for resolving the on-premises domain queries while still allowing Route 53 Resolver to handle other DNS requests by default forwarding them to the internet. Sharing the rule with the organization using AWS RAM simplifies deployment across all VPCs.

You cannot create a hosted zone (both private and public) for the amazonaws.com domain - these are reserved. So, the correct answers are B and D.

Reference:

Please refer the below extract taken from the link - https://aws.amazon.com/blogs/security/simplify-dns-management-in-a-multiaccount-environment-with-route-53-resolver/

"You can mount an Amazon EFS file system on an Amazon EC2 instance using DNS names. The file system DNS name automatically resolves to the mount target's IP address in the Availability Zone of the connecting Amazon EC2 instance. To be able to do that, the VPC must use the default DNS provided by Amazon to resolve EFS DNS names.

If you plan to use EFS in your environment, I recommend that you resolve EFS DNS names locally and avoid sending these queries to central DNS because clients in that case would not receive answers optimized for their availability zone, which might result in higher operation latencies and less durability."

So, option B) answers EFS resolution from VPC. Combination of Option B and D explains resolution from on-prem.

12) Correct answer: C. Create a Network Load Balancer (NLB). Add a TCP listener to the NLB. Configure the Auto Scaling group to register instances with the NLB's target group.

Based on the requirements given in the question, option C is the most suitable and correct solution. The Network Load Balancer (NLB) can handle TCP and UDP traffic, and it can also encrypt traffic with SSL/TLS encryption. Additionally, NLB is designed for high performance, low latency traffic and can handle millions of requests per second, making it well-suited for handling the continuously changing customer demand mentioned in the question.

Option A, creating an Application Load Balancer (ALB), is also a viable solution for load balancing traffic to the EC2 instances, but it may not be the best option for handling high volumes of TCP and UDP traffic, especially when it comes to real-time applications.

C covers the requirement for end-to-end encryption.

C is the only option that provides the connection from client not to be terminated in any intermediate point but the application server.

Reference:

If you need to pass encrypted traffic to the targets without the load balancer decrypting it, create a TCP listener on port 443 instead of creating a TLS listener.

https://docs.aws.amazon.com/elasticloadbalancing/latest/network/create-tls-listener.html

13) The correct answer to this question is option B: Change the router configurations to summarize the advertised routes.

Here's why:

The issue described in the question is that the VPC route table is not receiving all of the advertised routes from the on-premises routers. The router at the first location is advertising 110 routes, but those routes are n

You can announce a maximum of 100 prefixes to AWS. These routes can be automatically be propagated into subnet route tables.

• In order to advertise more than 100 prefixes, you should summarize the prefixes into larger range to reduce number of prefixes.

Reference:

https://docs.aws.amazon.com/directconnect/latest/UserGuide/limits.html

You can do a route summarization if you can or consider using Transit Gateway Connect to build an overlay GRE tunnel with BGP session to advertise your routing information.

14) The correct steps to meet these requirements are:

B. Create an Amazon Route 53 Resolver inbound endpoint in the shared account VPC. Create a conditional forwarder for a domain named aws.example.internal on the on-premises DNS servers. Set the forwarding IP addresses to the inbound endpoint's IP addresses that were created.

D. Create an Amazon Route 53 private hosted zone named aws.example.internal in the shared AWS account to resolve queries for this domain.

F. Create a private hosted zone in the shared AWS account for each account that runs the service. Configure the private hosted zone to contain aws.example.internal in the domain (account1.aws.example.internal). Associate the private hosted zone with the VPC that runs the service and the shared account VPC.

These steps allow service creators to manage their DNS records within their respective AWS accounts, simplifying the process and reducing the need for manual intervention and coordination among teams.

Inbound resolver endpoint and forwarder rule in on-premises DNS Servers, Private Hosted Zones for aws.example.internal and sub domain delegation to respective services (service<x>.aws.example.internal), and association the sub domain private hosted zones with respective VPCs in other accounts.

15) Correct answer: B. Modify the transit gateway VPC attachment on the shared services VPC by enabling appliance mode support.

Enabling appliance mode support on the transit gateway VPC

attachment helps in resolving the intermittent connection issues for traffic that crosses Availability Zones. Appliance mode support ensures that traffic is processed by the transit gateway appliance before being forwarded to its destination, which can help in maintaining consistent connectivity and routing behavior across Availability Zones.

Appliance mode should be enabled to ensure that the returning traffic (in case of stateful connections) takes the same path as incoming traffic, otherwise it might go to different AZs.

Please note: "IDS services for stateful inspection" - this implies the same appliance is followed for the life of the connection. This is only achieved by on the shared services VPC by enabling appliance mode support.

Reference:

https://docs.aws.amazon.com/vpc/latest/tgw/transit-gateway-appliance-scenario.html#transit-gateway-appliance-support

16) Correct answer: ACD

A. Validate that private DNS is enabled on the VPC by setting the enableDnsHostnames VPC attribute and the enableDnsSupport VPC attribute to true. This step ensures that the instances in the private subnets can resolve AWS service endpoints using private DNS.

C. Create a new security group with entries to allow inbound traffic that uses the TCP protocol on port 443 from the IP prefixes of the private subnets. This step allows the instances in the private subnets to communicate with the CloudWatch endpoints.

D. Create the following interface VPC endpoints in the

VPC: com.amazonaws.us-west-2.logs and com.amazonaws.us-west-2.monitoring. Associate the new security group with the endpoint network interfaces. This step creates VPC endpoints for CloudWatch Logs and CloudWatch Monitoring, allowing the CloudWatch agent to send logs and metrics data to CloudWatch without going through the NAT gateway.

These steps ensure that the CloudWatch agent can continue to function properly after the removal of the NAT gateway.

References:

An interface VPC endpoint provides reliable, scalable connectivity to CloudWatch without requiring a NAT gateway.

https://docs.aws.amazon.com/AmazonCloudWatch/latest/monitoring/cloudwatch-and-interface-VPC.html

https://docs.aws.amazon.com/vpc/latest/privatelink/aws-services-privatelink-support.html

To use private DNS, you must enable DNS hostnames and DNS resolution for your VPC.

The security group for the interface endpoint must allow communication between the endpoint network interface and the resources in your VPC that must communicate with the service.

https://docs.aws.amazon.com/vpc/latest/privatelink/create-interface-endpoint.html

https://docs.aws.amazon.com/vpc/latest/privatelink/aws-services-privatelink-support.html

17) The solution with the HIGHEST availability for connecting the globally distributed IoT devices to the AWS infrastructure

across multiple Regions is:

C. Set up an accelerator in AWS Global Accelerator. Configure Regional endpoint groups and health checks.

Here's why this option offers the highest availability:

Global Acceleration: AWS Global Accelerator provides a globally distributed network of edge locations that route traffic to the closest healthy endpoint, minimizing latency and improving overall performance.

Regional Endpoint Groups: By creating Regional endpoint groups for each Region where the solution is deployed, the network engineer can direct traffic to the most appropriate AWS infrastructure based on the device location.

Health Checks: Configuring health checks on the Regional endpoint groups ensures that only healthy endpoints (services running in the AWS Regions) receive traffic. If a Region experiences an outage, traffic will be automatically routed to the next closest healthy endpoint in another Region, minimizing downtime and data loss.

Let's explore why the other options might not offer the same level of availability:

A. CloudFront with Origin Failover (Limited Scope): CloudFront is a content delivery network (CDN) primarily used for distributing static content. While it can offer origin failover, it's not designed for real-time data transmissions like those from the IoT devices. Additionally, CloudFront doesn't inherently provide regional routing capabilities.

B. Route 53 Latency-Based Routing (DNS Resolution, Not High Availability): Route 53 latency-based routing helps direct users to the closest resources based on latency. However, it primarily focuses on DNS resolution, not necessarily ensuring high availability of the backend services themselves.

D. BYOIP Addresses (Limited Failover): While BYOIP allows using the company's PI addresses across Regions, it doesn't inherently provide automatic failover mechanisms for service outages within the AWS infrastructure.

Therefore, AWS Global Accelerator, with its combination of global edge locations, Regional endpoint groups, and health checks, offers a more comprehensive solution for high-availability routing of critical data from the geographically dispersed IoT devices to the company's AWS infrastructure across multiple Regions.

References:

https://docs.aws.amazon.com/global-accelerator/latest/dg/introduction-benefits-of-migrating.html

https://docs.aws.amazon.com/global-accelerator/latest/dg/using-byoip.html

18) The solution that achieves the highest throughput for encrypted data transfer during the migration while utilizing the established 10 Gbps AWS Direct Connect connection is:

C. Configure MACsec for the Direct Connect connection. Configure a transit VIF to a Direct Connect gateway that is associated with the transit gateway.

Here's why this option provides the highest throughput:

10 Gbps Direct Connect: The established connection offers a dedicated high-bandwidth path for data transfer.

MACsec Encryption: MACsec (Media Access Control Security)

provides line-rate encryption for the traffic on the Direct Connect link, ensuring data confidentiality without compromising performance. It operates at Layer 2, unlike traditional IPsec VPNs which operate at Layer 3 and can introduce overhead.

Transit VIF: Configuring a transit VIF on the Direct Connect connection allows routing traffic to the transit gateway, enabling centralized management and connection to multiple VPCs within the AWS environment.

Direct Connect Gateway with Transit Gateway: Associating the Direct Connect gateway with the transit gateway facilitates centralized route management and simplifies traffic flow to the desired VPCs.

Let's analyze why the other options might not be ideal for achieving the highest throughput:

A. Public VIF with Site-to-Site VPN: Public VIFs are not recommended for production environments due to security concerns. Site-to-Site VPNs, while offering encryption, can introduce overhead compared to MACsec, potentially impacting throughput, especially with a high-bandwidth connection like 10 Gbps.

B. Transit VIF with Third-Party VPN: While a transit VIF can be used with VPN connections, utilizing third-party VPN software on an EC2 instance can add complexity and might not be optimized for performance on a 10 Gbps connection compared to the native MACsec solution.

D. Public VIF with Dual VPNs and ECMP: ECMP (Equal-Cost Multi-Path) routing can potentially improve overall throughput by distributing traffic across both VPN connections. However, similar to option A, using public VIFs introduces security risks. Additionally, VPN overhead can still impact performance compared to MACsec.

Therefore, configuring MACsec encryption directly on the 10 Gbps Direct Connect connection offers the most streamlined and performant solution for secure and high-throughput data transfer during the critical workload migration to AWS.

Reference:

https://docs.aws.amazon.com/directconnect/latest/UserGuide/MACsec.html

19) The most likely solution for the network engineer to resolve the error and successfully provision the resources with CloudFormation is:

D. Add the DependsOn attribute to the resource declaration for the route table entry. Specify the virtual private gateway resource.

Here's why this approach addresses the potential issue:

Resource Dependencies: The virtual private gateway (VGW) needs to be created and operational before static routes can be added to a route table that references the VGW.

DependsOn Attribute: CloudFormation allows specifying dependencies between resources using the DependsOn attribute. This ensures that resources are created in the correct order to avoid errors during provisioning.

By adding the DependsOn attribute and specifying the VGW resource, the CloudFormation template instructs the service to wait for the VGW to be created and ready before attempting to configure the route table entry that references it. This helps prevent errors due to missing resources during the stack creation process.

Let's explore why the other options might not be the most effective solutions:

A. Changing Resource Creation Order (Unreliable): While changing the order might work occasionally, it's not a guaranteed solution. CloudFormation might have additional dependencies internally that the engineer might not be aware of.

B. DependsOn on VGW for Route Table (Incorrect Dependency): The route table itself might not directly depend on the VGW. The dependency lies within the route table entry that references the VGW for outbound traffic.

C. Wait Condition for VGW (Overly Broad): A wait condition can be useful, but waiting specifically for the VGW might be unnecessary if other resources are also involved. Focusing the wait on the resource directly referenced in the route table entry provides a more targeted approach.

Therefore, using the DependsOn attribute to specify the dependency between the route table entry and the VGW ensures the resources are provisioned in the correct sequence, resolving the error and allowing the CloudFormation stack to create the VPN connection successfully.

Route table route entry can't reference the VPG if it is not available.

References:

According to the below AWS document, you must configure your route table to include the routes used by your Site-to-Site VPN connection and point them to your virtual private gateway.

https://docs.aws.amazon.com/vpn/latest/s2svpn/SetUpVPNConnections.html

That means you must create the virtual private gateway before creating the route table.

AWS CloudFormation does not support configuring detailed run order of creating resources. However, when you add a DependsOn attribute to a resource, that resource is created only after the creation of the resource specified in the DependsOn attribute.

https://docs.aws.amazon.com/AWSCloudFormation/latest/UserGuide/aws-attribute-dependson.html

20) The modifications that will meet the requirements are:

C. Add the aggregate IP prefix for the other Region and the local VPC CIDR blocks to the list of subnets advertised through the local Direct Connect connection.

E. Remove all the VPC CIDR prefixes from the list of subnets advertised through the local Direct Connect connection. Add both Regional aggregate IP prefixes to the list of subnets advertised through the Direct Connect connection on both sides of the network. Configure data center routers to make routing decisions based on the BGP communities received.

Explanation:

Option C ensures that the aggregate IP prefix for the other Region and the local VPC CIDR blocks are advertised through the local Direct Connect connection, which allows the data center routers to learn routes to the other Region.

Option E further enhances this by removing the specific VPC CIDR prefixes from the Direct Connect connection advertisement and adding the Regional aggregate IP prefixes instead. This ensures that routing decisions can be made based on the received BGP communities, allowing for more efficient routing and cost minimization on AWS.

If the private WAN failed, the network engineer would swing the traffic to the other region through the local Direct Connect and the Transit Gateways. That is the requirement.

The solution is that the local DC has 2 kinds of route to the other region VPCs. One is the existing CIDR-based routes via the private WAN, another is the advertised aggregated routes from the local Direct Connect connection. CIDR-based routes are prior to the aggregated routes advertised from Direct Connect connection due to the longest prefix match routing algorithm.

The options which match this solution are C and E.

Reference:

Private virtual interface and transit virtual interface BGP communities

AWS Direct Connect supports local preference BGP community tags to help control the route preference of traffic on private virtual interfaces and transit virtual interfaces.

https://docs.aws.amazon.com/directconnect/latest/UserGuide/routing-and-bgp.html

21) The most suitable solution for the network engineer to address the limitations of a single EC2 instance overloaded by mirrored traffic while achieving high availability and scalability is:

A. Deploy a Network Load Balancer (NLB) as the traffic mirror target. Behind the NLB, deploy a fleet of EC2 instances in an Auto Scaling group. Use Traffic Mirroring as necessary.

Here's why this option meets the requirements:

Network Load Balancer (NLB): An NLB is ideal for distributing Layer 4 (TCP/UDP) traffic across multiple backend targets based on network connection information (IP address, port) without requiring complex health checks. This makes it suitable for mirrored traffic, which is typically unencrypted and relies on port information for identification.

Auto Scaling Group: Deploying a fleet of EC2 instances behind the NLB provides horizontal scaling. The Auto Scaling group can automatically scale the number of instances based on predefined metrics (e.g., CPU utilization) to handle increased traffic volume from mirrored sessions. This ensures the mirrored traffic is distributed and processed efficiently.

Traffic Mirroring as Needed: The network engineer can continue to utilize Traffic Mirroring to capture specific network traffic flows for analysis without compromising the solution's scalability.

Let's explore why the other options are not ideal solutions:

B. Application Load Balancer (Unnecessary Complexity): An ALB is designed for Layer 7 (HTTP/HTTPS) traffic and requires health checks on the backend instances. These features are not necessary for mirrored traffic, introducing unnecessary complexity. Additionally, limiting Traffic Mirroring to non-business hours might not capture critical security events.

C. Gateway Load Balancer (Limited Scope): A GLB is primarily used for routing traffic to multiple VPCs or on-premises networks. While it can distribute traffic, it's not specifically designed for the load balancing requirements of mirrored network traffic.

D. ALB with Limited Mirroring: Similar to option B, using an

ALB with an HTTPS listener adds unnecessary complexity for mirrored traffic. Restricting Traffic Mirroring to specific times might hinder security analysis efforts.

Therefore, the combination of an NLB for traffic distribution and an Auto Scaling group for horizontal scaling provides a highly available and scalable solution to handle the increased demand of mirrored traffic while maintaining the ability to use Traffic Mirroring as needed for security analysis.

Reference:

Traffic mirror target concepts:

A traffic mirror target is the destination for mirrored traffic.

You can use the following resources as traffic mirror targets:

- Network interfaces of type interface
- Network Load Balancers
- Gateway Load Balancer endpoints

https://docs.aws.amazon.com/vpc/latest/mirroring/traffic-mirroring-targets.html

22) Correct answer: BCE

The correct combination of steps for the network engineer to take in order to replace the open-source recursive DNS resolver with Amazon Route 53 Resolver endpoints are:

B. Configure the on-premises DNS resolver to forward aws.example.com domain queries to the IP addresses of the inbound endpoint. This ensures that requests for the aws.example.com domain from the on-premises DNS resolver are directed to the Route 53 Resolver inbound endpoint for resolution.

C. Create a Route 53 Resolver inbound endpoint and a Route 53 Resolver outbound endpoint. This is necessary to establish communication between the on-premises DNS resolver and the VPC's DNS resolver.

E. Create a Route 53 Resolver rule to forward corp.example.com domain queries to the IP address of the on-premises DNS resolver. This ensures that requests for the corp.example.com domain from the VPC's DNS resolver are forwarded to the on-premises DNS resolver.

These steps will allow for the successful replacement of the open-source recursive DNS resolver with Amazon Route 53 Resolver endpoints while maintaining communication between the on-premises and VPC environments.

Reference:

https://docs.aws.amazon.com/Route53/latest/DeveloperGuide/resolver.html

23) Correct answer: BC

The key requirements for the government contractor's solution involve high availability, automated failover, and preventing asymmetric routing in a multi-account environment with a third-party inspection appliance. Here are the two most suitable approaches:

B. Gateway Load Balancer (GLB) with Network Load Balancer (NLB) for HA and Inspection:

Inspection VPC and Appliance Deployment: Deploy two clusters of inspection appliances across multiple Availability Zones within a designated inspection VPC. This provides redundancy and fault tolerance.

Transit Gateway Connectivity: Connect the inspection VPC to the transit gateway using a VPC attachment.

Target Group and NLB: Create a target group in a single account and register the inspection appliances (from both clusters) with the target group. This ensures all appliances are eligible for traffic distribution.

Gateway Load Balancer: Create a Gateway Load Balancer (GLB) and configure it to forward traffic to the target group containing the inspection appliances. The GLB operates across accounts, making it suitable for a multi-account environment.

Route Table Configuration: In the inspection VPC's transit gateway subnet, configure a default route pointing to the GLB endpoint. This ensures traffic from all VPC attachments reaches the inspection tier via the NLB and target group.

This configuration leverages the NLB for efficient traffic distribution within the inspection VPC and the GLB for cross-account routing between application VPCs and the inspection tier. Additionally, registering all appliances in a single target group prevents asymmetric routing, where traffic might bypass inspection through a specific appliance.

C. Transit Gateway Appliance Mode with Static Routes:

Route Tables: Configure two separate route tables on the transit gateway.

One route table associates with all the application VPC attachments.

The other route table associates with the inspection VPC attachment.

Route Propagation: Propagate all VPC attachments (including the inspection VPC) into the application route table. This ensures all VPCs can reach each other through the transit gateway.

Static Routes: Define a static default route in the inspection route table, pointing the traffic towards the inspection appliances within the VPC (potentially using an internal load balancer for distribution within the inspection VPC).

Appliance Mode: Enable appliance mode on the attachment that connects the inspection VPC to the transit gateway. This ensures traffic destined for other VPCs is routed through the inspection appliances.

This approach utilizes static routes and appliance mode to achieve traffic inspection. However, it requires careful route table configuration and might not offer the same level of dynamic load balancing and automated failover compared to the solution with a Network Load Balancer and Gateway Load Balancer combination.

Let's explore why the other options are not ideal solutions:

A. NLB with Target Group (Limited Scalability): While an NLB can distribute traffic within a VPC, it's not ideal for cross-account routing in a multi-account environment. A Gateway Load Balancer is better suited for this purpose.

D. Static Route in Application Table (Incorrect Targeting): Defining a static route in the application route table directing traffic to the inspection appliances might not be optimal. This approach requires additional configuration on the inspection VPC side and might not be as dynamic as using appliance mode.

E. Single Route Table (Security Risk): Having a single route table with all VPC attachments can be a security risk, as a compromised route could potentially route traffic unexpectedly. Separate route tables provide better isolation and control.

References:

https://docs.aws.amazon.com/elasticloadbalancing/latest/gateway/introduction.html

https://docs.aws.amazon.com/whitepapers/latest/building-scalable-secure-multi-vpc-network-infrastructure/using-gwlb-with-tg-for-cns.html

24) The solution that will meet the requirements with the least amount of operational overhead is:

C. Deploy a NAT gateway into a private subnet in the VPC where the EC2 instances are deployed. Specify the NAT gateway type as private. Configure the on-premises firewall to allow connections from the IP address that is assigned to the NAT gateway.

Explanation:

Using a NAT gateway allows the EC2 instances to initiate outbound requests while keeping them hidden behind a single IP address.

The NAT gateway simplifies the setup compared to a NAT instance, as it is a managed service and does not require the same level of maintenance and monitoring.

Configuring the on-premises firewall to allow connections from the IP address of the NAT gateway simplifies the firewall rules, as it only requires allowing traffic from a single IP address.

Reference:

You need a NAT:

https://docs.aws.amazon.com/vpc/latest/userguide/vpc-nat-gateway.html

25) The correct solution that meets the requirements for simplifying the network architecture, allowing for future growth, and migrating the production environments to AWS is:

C. Create a transit gateway in each Region with multiple new VPN connections from each data center. Share the transit gateways with each account using AWS Resource Access Manager (AWS RAM). In each Region, connect the transit gateway to each VPC. Remove existing VPN connections directly attached to the virtual private gateways.

Explanation:

Creating a transit gateway in each Region allows for a scalable and simplified network architecture, providing a centralized hub for connecting multiple VPCs and on-premises data centers.

Sharing the transit gateways with each account using AWS RAM simplifies management and allows for easy sharing of resources across multiple AWS accounts.

Connecting the transit gateway to each VPC in each Region provides a centralized point for routing traffic between the VPCs and on-premises data centers.

Removing existing VPN connections directly attached to the virtual private gateways reduces management overhead and simplifies the network configuration.

References:

An AWS Transit Gateway provides the option of creating an IPsec VPN connection between your remote network and the Transit Gateway over the internet. A Transit Gateway is a regional resource.

https://docs.aws.amazon.com/whitepapers/latest/aws-vpc-connectivity-options/aws-transit-gateway-vpn.html

You can use AWS Resource Access Manager (RAM) to share a transit gateway for VPC attachments across accounts or across your organization in AWS Organizations. That helps reducing the VPN connections.

https://docs.aws.amazon.com/vpc/latest/tgw/transit-gateway-share.html

AWS Transit Gateway can scale up to 50 Gbps throughput aggregating multiple VPN tunnels.

https://docs.aws.amazon.com/vpc/latest/tgw/transit-gateway-quotas.html#bandwidth-quotas

Option A may be a stable solution considering other options, but will not be applicable to this scenario as a single Direct connect gateway can connect only up to 10 VPCs, whereas the requirement states total 120 VPCs. This choice would have been applicable had Transit Gateway been introduced to the architecture with Transit VIF (not private VIF).

As Transit gateway is a regional resource, a single transit gateway will not function cross-region.

26) The best solution to meet these requirements and reduce NAT gateway costs is:

D. Implement gateway VPC endpoints for Amazon S3. Update the VPC route table.

Explanation:

Gateway VPC Endpoints for Amazon S3: By creating a gateway VPC endpoint for Amazon S3, you can ensure that traffic between your EC2 instances and the S3 bucket remains within the AWS network. This eliminates the need for traffic to pass through a NAT gateway, thereby reducing costs.

Update the VPC Route Table: Once the gateway VPC endpoint is created, you need to update the VPC route table to route traffic destined for Amazon S3 through the endpoint. This configuration ensures that all requests to S3 are handled internally by the VPC, without traversing the public internet or a NAT gateway.

Cost Efficiency: Using gateway VPC endpoints for S3 is cost-effective as it does not incur data transfer charges that NAT gateways would, significantly reducing the overall costs associated with S3 access from within your VPC.

This solution is optimal as it directly addresses the issue of high costs associated with the NAT gateway and provides a seamless, secure, and cost-effective way for EC2 instances to access S3 buckets.

Reference:

https://aws.amazon.com/premiumsupport/knowledge-center/vpc-reduce-nat-gateway-transfer-costs/

Determine whether the majority of your NAT gateway charges are from traffic to Amazon Simple Storage Service or Amazon DynamoDB in the same Region. If they are, then set up a gateway VPC endpoint. Route traffic to and from the AWS resource through the gateway VPC endpoint, rather than through the NAT gateway. There are no processing or hourly charges for using gateway VPC endpoints.

27) The most suitable solution for the network engineer to gain visibility into new route advertisements from the on-premises network to AWS and trigger notifications is:

B. Leverage Transit Gateway Network Manager with CloudWatch Logs Insights and Amazon EventBridge:

Here's why this approach effectively meets the requirements:

Transit Gateway Network Manager: Onboarding the transit gateway to Transit Gateway Network Manager provides a centralized view of routing information within the transit gateway, including routes learned from the on-premises network via Direct Connect.

CloudWatch Logs Insights: Enable CloudWatch Logs Insights for Transit Gateway Network Manager logs. This allows for querying and analyzing the log data to identify new route advertisements.

Amazon EventBridge (CloudWatch Events): Create a CloudWatch rule in Amazon EventBridge based on a filter expression within CloudWatch Logs Insights. This filter can identify entries indicating new route advertisements in the Transit Gateway Network Manager logs.

Notifications: Configure Amazon EventBridge to trigger specific actions upon detecting new route advertisements, such as sending notifications through email, SMS, or other desired channels.

Let's explore why the other options are not ideal solutions:

A. CloudWatch Metrics on Direct Connect (Limited Visibility): CloudWatch metrics on Direct Connect offer general connection health and performance information but might not provide specific details on advertised routes.

C. Lambda Function Polling (Manual Work and Inefficiency): Setting up a Lambda function to periodically check routes on the Direct Connect gateway introduces manual work and potential inefficiencies. Additionally, Lambda functions might not be cost-effective for continuous monitoring.

D. CloudWatch Logs on Transit VIFs (Incomplete Information): CloudWatch Logs on transit VIFs might not capture all routing information, especially routes learned from the on-premises network.

By leveraging Transit Gateway Network Manager for centralized routing visibility, CloudWatch Logs Insights for log analysis, and Amazon EventBridge for event-driven notifications, the network engineer establishes an automated and efficient solution for monitoring new route advertisements and triggering alerts.

Transit Gateway Network Manager provides a centralized view of global networks built on AWS Transit Gateway. It also provides the capability to monitor the routing tables associated with the transit gateway, and then forward routing information to CloudWatch Logs Insights. Once in CloudWatch Logs Insights, you can use EventBridge rules to trigger notifications based on routing changes. This will allow the company to receive notifications each time a new route is advertised to AWS from on-premises over Direct Connect, which meets the requirements. The other options either do not provide the necessary functionality or would not be the most efficient solution for this scenario.

Reference:

https://docs.aws.amazon.com/network-manager/latest/cloudwan/cloudwan-cloudwatch-events.html

28) The most efficient solution for the software company to achieve encryption for traffic between AWS and the colocation

facility while maintaining existing bandwidth and minimizing operational overhead is:

C. Leverage New Direct Connect Connections with MACsec:

Here's why this approach offers the least operational overhead:

New Direct Connect Connections with MACsec: Establish two new 10 Gbps Direct Connect connections with MACsec enabled. MACsec is a Layer 2 encryption standard that operates efficiently on existing high-bandwidth connections. This provides encryption without sacrificing bandwidth compared to the existing Direct Connect setup.

Edge Router Configuration: Configure MACsec on the edge routers within the colocation facility to match the settings on the AWS side of the Direct Connect connections. This establishes the secure tunnel for encrypted communication.

Traffic Rerouting: Reroute traffic from the existing Direct Connect private VIFs to the new MACsec-enabled Direct Connect connections. This ensures all traffic leverages the encryption capabilities.

Decommission Original Connections: Once traffic is successfully routed through the new encrypted connections, decommission the original Direct Connect connections.

Let's explore why the other options might introduce more operational overhead:

A. New Public VIF with Encryption (Unnecessary Complexity): Creating a new public VIF with encryption adds unnecessary complexity. Direct Connect with MACsec already provides Layer 2 encryption without requiring a separate public VIF.

B. VPN Connections (Lower Bandwidth and Overhead): Establishing Site-to-Site VPN connections would introduce

103

additional overhead compared to the existing Direct Connect setup. VPNs typically offer lower bandwidth compared to dedicated Direct Connect connections. Additionally, managing and maintaining VPN tunnels might require more effort.

D. New Connections with VPNs (Redundant Complexity): This option involves deploying new Direct Connect connections with MACsec, similar to the recommended approach (C). However, it adds unnecessary complexity by also creating Site-to-Site VPN connections on top of the new public VIFs. VPNs are not required for encryption when using MACsec with Direct Connect.

By leveraging new Direct Connect connections with MACsec, the software company achieves its encryption goals while maintaining current bandwidth and minimizing the need for additional configuration or management overhead on the existing infrastructure.

References:

https://docs.aws.amazon.com/directconnect/latest/ UserGuide/MACsec.html

"You can use AWS Direct Connect connections that support MACsec to encrypt your data from your on-premises network or collocated device to your chosen AWS Direct Connect point of presence".

https://aws.amazon.com/directconnect/faqs/

29) The most operationally efficient solution to collect and analyze access logs containing client IP, target IP, target port, and user agent for the application behind the ALB is:

D. Configure ALB to store logs in S3 and use Athena for analysis.

Here's why this approach offers the best operational efficiency:

ALB Log Delivery to S3: Configure the ALB to store access logs in an Amazon S3 bucket. This is a straightforward setup and avoids manual download processes.

Athena for Log Analysis: Use Amazon Athena, a serverless interactive query service, to analyze the logs stored in S3. Athena allows querying data in S3 using standard SQL syntax, making it user-friendly for analysts to filter and analyze relevant access logs without needing to download or transform the data.

This approach minimizes operational overhead by leveraging managed services and avoiding manual data manipulation.

Let's explore why the other options might involve more operational complexity:

A. Downloading & Manual Analysis (Inefficient and Error Prone): Downloading S3 files and using spreadsheets for analysis is a manual and time-consuming process. It might also be error-prone when dealing with large datasets.

B. Kinesis Data Streams & Kinesis Data Analytics (Redundant Processing): While Kinesis Data Streams can ingest ALB logs, using Kinesis Data Analytics for further analysis adds another layer of processing and configuration. Athena can directly query data in S3, eliminating the need for this intermediate step.

C. Kinesis Data Streams & OpenSearch Service (Complex Pipeline): This option involves streaming data through Kinesis Data Streams and then into OpenSearch Service (a search and analytics engine). While powerful, setting up and managing this pipeline might be more complex than using Athena for direct S3 query access.

By leveraging ALB log delivery to S3 and subsequent analysis with Athena, the network engineer achieves efficient log collection and analysis without extensive manual intervention or complex data pipelines. This allows for faster and more streamlined investigation of user access patterns following the security breach.

References:

https://docs.aws.amazon.com/elasticloadbalancing/latest/application/load-balancer-access-logs.html

https://repost.aws/knowledge-center/athena-analyze-access-logs

30) To meet the security requirement of encrypting traffic in transit at all times between the users and the backend, the company must make the following changes:

Correct Answers:

B, D, E.

Explanation:

B. Create a certificate for service.example.com by using AWS Certificate Manager (ACM). Configure CloudFront to use this custom SSL/TLS certificate. Change the default behavior to redirect HTTP to HTTPS.

This step ensures that traffic between the users and CloudFront is encrypted. Using ACM to create the certificate for service.example.com provides a managed and secure way to handle SSL/TLS certificates. Configuring CloudFront to use this certificate ensures that HTTPS is used for all user connections.

D. Create a public certificate from a third-party certificate provider with any domain name for the EC2 instances. Configure the backend to use this certificate for its HTTPS listener. Specify the instance target type during the creation of a new target group that uses the HTTPS protocol for its targets. Attach the existing Auto Scaling group to this new target group.

This step ensures that the communication between the ALB and the EC2 instances is encrypted. Configuring the backend (EC2 instances) to use HTTPS with a certificate ensures that all internal traffic within the VPC is also encrypted, providing end-to-end encryption.

E. Create a certificate for service-alb.example.com by using AWS Certificate Manager (ACM). On the ALB add a new HTTPS listener that uses the new target group and the service-alb.example.com ACM certificate. Modify the CloudFront origin to use the HTTPS protocol only. Delete the HTTP listener on the ALB.

This step ensures that traffic between CloudFront and the ALB is encrypted. By using ACM to create a certificate for service-alb.example.com and adding an HTTPS listener on the ALB, you ensure that the communication between CloudFront and the ALB is secure. Modifying the CloudFront origin to use HTTPS only and deleting the HTTP listener on the ALB enforces encryption throughout the entire path.

These steps collectively ensure that all segments of the network path from the user to the backend application are encrypted, thus meeting the company's security policy requirements.

References:

ACM removes the time-consuming manual process of purchasing, uploading, and renewing SSL/TLS certificates.

https://aws.amazon.com/certificate-manager/

https://docs.aws.amazon.com/AmazonCloudFront/latest/DeveloperGuide/cnames-and-https-requirements.html

https://docs.aws.amazon.com/elasticloadbalancing/latest/application/create-https-listener.html

You can configure one or more cache behaviors in your CloudFront distribution to require HTTPS for communication between viewers and CloudFront.

https://docs.aws.amazon.com/AmazonCloudFront/latest/DeveloperGuide/using-https-viewers-to-cloudfront.html

Option C is wrong. You cannot associate ACM certificates with an EC2 instance that is not connected to a Nitro Enclave.

https://docs.aws.amazon.com/acm/latest/userguide/acm-services.html

31) Correct answer: A. Enable the new Availability Zone on the NLB.

The Network Load Balancer (NLB) needs to be configured to recognize and utilize the new Availability Zone. By enabling the new Availability Zone on the NLB, the load balancer will start distributing traffic to instances in both Availability Zones, providing improved availability and load balancing.

Option B suggests creating a new NLB, which is not necessary in this scenario. NLBs are designed to distribute traffic across instances in multiple Availability Zones, and adding the new

Availability Zone to the existing NLB is the appropriate step.

Options C and D are not directly addressing the issue. Enabling proxy protocol (Option C) is useful for passing client information to the backend servers, but it doesn't resolve the issue of traffic not being routed to instances in the second Availability Zone. Creating a new target group (Option D) might be necessary for specific use cases, but it doesn't directly address the problem in this context.

Reference:

"You can't disable Availability Zones for a Network Load Balancer after you create it, but you can enable additional Availability Zones."

https://docs.aws.amazon.com/elasticloadbalancing/latest/network/network-load-balancers.html#availability-zones

32) The most suitable approach for the network engineer to configure a launch template for the Auto Scaling group with a secondary network interface using a BYOIP address is:

D. User Data Script with BYOIP Allocation:

Here's why this approach effectively meets the requirements:

Launch Template Configuration: Within the launch template, configure the primary network interface to be placed in a private subnet as needed.

User Data Script: Utilize the user data option to execute a cloud-init script after the instance boots up. This script can be used to achieve the following:

Attach Secondary Interface: The script can programmatically attach a new network interface to the instance.

BYOIP Allocation: The script can leverage the AWS CLI or SDK to associate an Elastic IP address from the designated BYOIP pool with the newly attached secondary network interface. This ensures the network appliance receives the desired public IP address for application traffic.

This approach provides a flexible and automated way to configure the secondary interface and assign the BYOIP address during the instance launch process.

Let's explore why the other options are less ideal:

A. Launch Template Interface Configuration (Limited Functionality): While the launch template allows configuring network interfaces, it cannot directly associate Elastic IP addresses from BYOIP pools. User data scripts offer more flexibility for dynamic configuration tasks.

B. User Data Script with Auto-assigned IP (Incorrect Addressing): Using user data to attach a second interface with auto-assigned public IP addressing from a public subnet wouldn't leverage the BYOIP pool and wouldn't meet the requirement of using a specific Elastic IP address.

C. Lambda Function as Lifecycle Hook (Overly Complex): Developing a Lambda function as a lifecycle hook for assigning a network interface to a Global Accelerator endpoint is not necessary for this scenario. The focus is on attaching a secondary interface and associating a BYOIP address, which can be achieved with a user data script.

References:

https://aws.amazon.com/about-aws/whats-new/2020/11/amazon-ec2-auto-scaling-supports-attaching-multiple-network-interfaces-at-launch/

https://repost.aws/knowledge-center/ec2-auto-scaling-multiple-network-interfaces

33) Correct answer: BCD

The network engineer needs to achieve two key goals:

Internal DNS resolution: The application components within the VPC need to resolve hostnames using the same names used publicly, but pointing to the private IPs of the backend components.

Dynamic updates: The solution should allow for future additions or removals of DNS entries without manual configuration for each change.

Here's why only three options meet these requirements:

A. Geoproximity routing policy: This is not relevant for internal DNS resolution within the VPC.

B. Create a Route 53 private hosted zone: This creates a separate zone for internal resolution using the same domain name.

C. Enable DNS hostnames for the application's VPC: This allows instances within the VPC to use Route 53 for DNS resolution.

D. Create entries in the private zone with private IPs: This maps the public hostnames to the private IPs for internal resolution.

E. EventBridge and Lambda for updates: This could automate updates for the private zone, but it's an overly complex approach for this scenario.

F. Add private IPs to the public zone: This would expose private IPs publicly, defeating the purpose of a private zone.

Therefore, the best combination of steps is:

B. Create a Route 53 private hosted zone for the same domain name.

C. Enable DNS hostnames for the application's VPC.

D. Create entries in the private zone with private IPs.

This configuration allows internal components to resolve hostnames using the public names while pointing to the private backend servers. Option E offers automation but is unnecessarily complex for this situation. Option F compromises security by exposing private IPs publicly.

Reference:

https://docs.aws.amazon.com/vpc/latest/userguide/vpc-dns.html#vpc-dns-hostnames

"If you use custom DNS domain names defined in a private hosted zone in Amazon Route 53, or use private DNS with interface VPC endpoints (AWS PrivateLink), you must set both the enableDnsHostnames and enableDnsSupport attributes to true."

34) D is correct: Choose a Network Load Balancer (NLB) as the type of load balancer for the ECS service. Specify the NLB in the service definition. Create a VPC endpoint service for the NLB. Share the VPC endpoint service with other AWS accounts.

Explanation:

Network Load Balancer (NLB): NLB is designed to handle millions of requests per second while maintaining ultra-low latencies. It is ideal for applications requiring high performance and low latency, which is important for SSL connections.

VPC Endpoint Service: Creating a VPC endpoint service for the

NLB and sharing it with other AWS accounts allows traffic to flow privately and securely from these accounts. This setup meets the requirement for private connectivity.

Manageable Scaling: NLBs are highly scalable and can automatically handle the increase in traffic as more consumers use the application. This ensures that the application scales in a manageable way without additional configuration or complexity.

Why other options are less suitable:

Option A (Gateway Load Balancer): While a Gateway Load Balancer is useful for distributing traffic to network appliances, it is not designed for application traffic and does not support SSL termination or advanced routing needed for this use case.

Option B (Application Load Balancer): Although ALB supports path-based routing and SSL termination, it does not provide the same level of performance and scalability as NLB for handling large volumes of SSL traffic.

Option C (ALB with VPC Peering): This setup involves more complexity in managing VPC peering connections and route table updates, which is less efficient compared to using a VPC endpoint service. Additionally, ALB is less suitable for high-performance, low-latency requirements compared to NLB.

Path based routing is not required here. Requirement is "Traffic must be able to flow to the application from other AWS accounts over private connectivity. " - which is a case for PrivateLink.

B - You cannot create a service endpoint for an ALB

Endpoint services require either a Network Load Balancer or a Gateway Load Balancer. The load balancer receives requests from service consumers and routes them to your service.

Reference:

https://docs.aws.amazon.com/vpc/latest/privatelink/create-endpoint-service.html

You can have the ALB behind the NLB but not directly as a service endpoint

35) C is correct: Create a VPC endpoint service. Associate the VPC endpoint service with the NLB for the web service. Create an interface VPC endpoint for the web service in the existing production VPC.

Explanation:

VPC Endpoint Service: By creating a VPC endpoint service and associating it with the NLB, you allow private connectivity from other VPCs to your web service without traversing the public internet. This provides a secure and scalable solution.

Interface VPC Endpoint: Creating an interface VPC endpoint in the existing production VPC allows instances in the production VPC to communicate with the web service via private IP addresses. This method ensures low latency and secure communication.

Minimal Disruption: This solution integrates the systems with minimal changes to the existing architecture. It avoids the need for significant reconfiguration or redeployment of the existing production environment.

Why other options are less suitable:

Option A (VPC Peering): While VPC peering is effective, it requires route table updates and security group adjustments, which can be more complex and riskier to implement on short notice.

Option B (Redeploying the Web Service): Redeploying the web service in the production VPC is disruptive and time-consuming, especially with a tight deadline.

Option D (Transit Gateway): Although a transit gateway is a powerful solution for connecting multiple VPCs, it introduces unnecessary complexity and cost for this scenario, where only two VPCs need to be connected for a specific use case.

The CIDR ranges are overlapping, hence VPC peering or Transit Gateway will not work in this scenario.

36) Correct answer: A. Update the Direct Connect transit VIF and configure BGP peering with the AWS assigned IPv6 peering address. Create a new VPN connection that supports IPv6 connectivity. Add an egress-only internet gateway. Update any affected VPC security groups and route tables to provide connectivity within the VPC and between the VPC and the on-premises devices

The MOST operationally efficient solution that meets the requirements is option A. This option updates the Direct Connect transit VIF to support IPv6 and configures BGP peering with the AWS assigned IPv6 peering address. It also creates a new VPN connection that supports IPv6 connectivity, adds an egress-only internet gateway, and updates any affected VPC security groups and route tables to provide connectivity within the VPC and between the VPC and the on-premises devices. This solution does not require any changes to the current infrastructure and effectively blocks direct access to the instances' new IPv6 addresses from the internet while allowing outbound internet access from the instances.

Reference:

https://aws.amazon.com/blogs/networking-and-content-delivery/dual-stack-ipv6-architectures-for-aws-an d-hybrid-networks/

For dual-stack connectivity on the Site-to-Site VPN connection via a Transit Gateway, you need to create two VPN connections, one for the IPv4 stack and one for the IPv6 stack. D. For AWS Direct Connect connection, reuse your existing VIFs and enable them for dual-stack support.

37) The most effective way to achieve perfect forward secrecy (PFS) with an ALB involves utilizing the built-in capabilities:

D. Change the ALB security policy to a policy that supports forward secrecy (FS)

Here's why the other options are not optimal solutions:

A. TLS 1.2 protocol: While TLS 1.2 is a more secure protocol than older versions, it alone doesn't guarantee PFS.

B. AWS KMS: AWS KMS is for managing encryption keys, but it doesn't directly implement PFS on ALBs.

C. WAF web ACL with FS rule: AWS WAF web ACLs are for filtering web requests and wouldn't directly enforce PFS on the ALB.

Forward secrecy (FS) is a cryptographic property that ensures even if an attacker compromises the server's long-term secret key, they cannot decrypt previously intercepted communications because each session uses a unique, temporary key.

Modern ALBs support TLS protocols that achieve PFS, such as

TLS 1.2 with Ephemeral Diffie-Hellman (ECDHE) key exchange. By selecting a security policy that enforces these protocols, the network engineer can leverage the built-in functionality of the ALB to achieve the desired outcome.

Use ELBSecurityPolicy-FS policies, if you require Forward Secrecy

• Provides additional safeguards against the eavesdropping of encrypted data.

• Using a unique random session key.

References:

Perfect Forward Secrecy is a feature that provides additional safeguards against the eavesdropping of encrypted data, through the use of a unique random session key. This prevents the decoding of captured data, even if the secret long-term key is compromised.

https://aws.amazon.com/about-aws/whats-new/2014/02/19/elastic-load-balancing-perfect-forward-secrecy-and-more-new-security-features/

https://aws.amazon.com/about-aws/whats-new/2018/06/application-load-balancer-adds-new-security-policies-including-policy-for-forward-secrecy/

38) Correct answer: C. Configure the AS_PATH prepend attribute on the secondary SD-WAN virtual appliance for BGP routes toward the transit gateway.

The key requirement is to ensure only one SD-WAN virtual appliance processes traffic from AWS workloads at a time, adhering to the company policy. Let's analyze the options:

A. Static route with more specific prefixes: This wouldn't achieve the desired outcome. More specific routes would override the default route, potentially causing all traffic to flow through the primary SD-WAN even for failover scenarios.

B. BGP community tag: While BGP communities can be used for route filtering, they are not ideal for controlling primary/secondary paths in this scenario.

C. AS_PATH prepend: This is the most suitable approach. By prepending the AS_PATH attribute on the secondary SD-WAN, the transit gateway will perceive those routes as less favorable compared to the routes from the primary SD-WAN. This will steer traffic towards the primary path most of the time.

D. Disabling ECMP: ECMP (Equal-Cost Multi-Path) allows load balancing across equal-cost paths. Disabling it might force all traffic to a single path, but it wouldn't guarantee which appliance (primary or secondary) would handle the traffic.

Therefore, configuring the AS_PATH prepend attribute on the secondary SD-WAN virtual appliance (Option C) is the most effective way to achieve the desired routing behavior while adhering to the company's policy of having only one active path for AWS traffic at a time. This approach leverages BGP routing mechanisms for path control.

Extra explanation:

A - incorrect, static routes are not possible in TGW

B- incorrect, these BGP communities are used for BGP over DX

C- correct, AS_PATH prepending is a standard BGP way of influencing return traffic for advertised prefixes and SDWAN supports this.

D- incorrect, disabling ECMP will make sure the SDWAN>TGW traffic is not load shared, but the return traffic TGW>SDWAN is not affected and therefore both appliances will process traffic.

Reference:

https://docs.aws.amazon.com/whitepapers/latest/aws-vpc-connectivity-options/aws-transit-gateway-sd-wan.html

SD-Wan connects to TGW using BGP for routing.

Therefore, no static route, therefore C is the answer.

39) Correct answer: B. Assign a new CIDR block to the transit gateway. Create a new VPC for the SD-WAN hub virtual appliance. Attach the new VPC to the transit gateway with a VPC attachment. Add a transit gateway Connect attachment. Create a Connect peer and specify the GRE and BGP parameters. Create a route in the appropriate VPC for the SD-WAN hub virtual appliance to route to the transit gateway.

The key requirement here is achieving a minimum throughput of 5 Gbps between the SD-WAN hub and other VPCs. Let's analyze the options based on this requirement:

A. Dual IPsec VPNs: IPsec VPNs typically have lower throughput compared to GRE tunnels used in Transit Gateway Connect. While BGP can be configured, it wouldn't address the core limitation of throughput with VPNs.

B. Transit Gateway Connect with GRE and BGP: This is the best solution. Transit Gateway Connect offers GRE tunnels which can achieve higher Throughput (up to 20 Gbps with four Connect peers) compared to IPsec VPNs. Additionally, BGP provides dynamic routing for optimal path selection.

C. Dual IPsec VPNs with BGP: Similar to A, this option wouldn't meet the high-throughput requirement.

D. Transit Gateway Connect with VXLAN: VXLAN is not supported by Transit Gateway Connect. It uses GRE tunnels for communication. While VXLAN can be used in other AWS services, it's not applicable here.

Therefore, the most suitable solution is B. Transit Gateway Connect with GRE and BGP. This configuration leverages the high-throughput capabilities of GRE tunnels and the routing flexibility of BGP to meet the 5 Gbps minimum throughput requirement.

A Connect attachment uses an existing VPC or AWS Direct Connect attachment as the underlying transport mechanism.

• Supports Generic Routing Encapsulation (GRE) tunnel protocol for high performance, and Border Gateway Protocol (BGP) for dynamic routing.

Reference:

https://aws.amazon.com/blogs/networking-and-content-delivery/simplify-sd-wan-connectivity-with-aws-transit-gateway-connect/

40) Correct answer: C. Establish an Internet Group Management Protocol (IGMP) multicast domain within the transit gateway. Associate the VPCs and relevant subnets with the multicast domain. Register the network interface of the multicast senders with the multicast domain. Modify the network ACLs to permit UDP traffic from the source to all receivers and UDP traffic sent to the multicast group address.

The key requirement here is dynamic multicasting with IGMP for automatic group membership management. Let's analyze the options:

A. Static source multicast domain: This wouldn't allow dynamic registration of receivers as required.

B. Static source multicast domain with TCP traffic: Multicast uses UDP, not TCP, for efficient data delivery.

C. IGMP multicast domain with UDP traffic: This is the most suitable approach. IGMP (Internet Group Management Protocol) enables dynamic membership in multicast groups. Associating VPCs and subnets with the IGMP domain allows receivers to join and leave multicast groups. Permitting UDP traffic allows for multicast communication within the VPCs.

D. IGMP multicast domain with TCP traffic: Similar to B, multicast uses UDP for efficient data delivery.

Therefore, the solution that meets the requirements for dynamic multicasting with IGMP is C.

References:

https://docs.aws.amazon.com/vpc/latest/tgw/how-multicast-works.html

https://docs.aws.amazon.com/vpc/latest/tgw/working-with-multicast.html#multicast-configurations-igmp

41) Correct answer: BE

B. Retrieve client IP addresses by using the X-Forwarded-For header.

E. Use an Application Load Balancer.

The scenario requires a load balancer that supports:

HTTPS termination: This eliminates Network Load Balancer

(NLB) as it operates at Layer 4 (TCP/UDP) and cannot handle SSL termination.

Client IP capture: The source IP address needs to be retrieved from the request headers.

Let's analyze the options:

A. Network Load Balancer (NLB): Not suitable due to lack of SSL termination.

B. X-Forwarded-For header: This is a standard header used by many proxies to record the client's IP address. It's a valid option for retrieving the source IP.

C. AWS App Mesh load balancing: While App Mesh can handle service discovery and routing for microservices, it doesn't directly provide load balancing functionality. It can be used in conjunction with an Application Load Balancer (ALB) for service mesh capabilities.

D. X-IP-Source header: This header is less commonly used than X-Forwarded-For, but it can also be used to retrieve the client's IP address.

E. Application Load Balancer (ALB): This is the most suitable load balancer. ALB supports:

HTTPS termination: It can terminate SSL/TLS connections, decrypting incoming traffic and encrypting outgoing traffic.

Client IP capture: ALB captures the client's IP address and adds it to the request headers, typically in the X-Forwarded-For header.

Therefore, the best approach is to combine:

B. Retrieve client IP addresses by using the X-Forwarded-For header: This captures the client's IP address for security and analytics purposes.

E. Use an Application Load Balancer (ALB): This fulfills the HTTPS termination requirement.

While D (X-IP-Source) is also technically an option for retrieving the IP address, X-Forwarded-For is a more widely used standard.

Reference:

https://docs.aws.amazon.com/elasticloadbalancing/latest/application/x-forwarded-headers.html

42) Correct answer: C. Create a VPC peering connection between the ingress VPC and each of the 10 services VPCs. Use zonal DNS names for the NLB in the services VPCs to minimize cross-AZ traffic from the ingress VPC to the services VPCs.

The key requirement here is minimizing data transfer costs between VPCs for a high volume of traffic (10 TB/month). Let's analyze the options based on data transfer pricing:

A. Transit Gateway: While it simplifies routing, transit gateway incurs data transfer charges within the AWS Region. This could be significant for a high data volume.

B. AWS PrivateLink: This eliminates internet data transfer charges but incurs AWS PrivateLink endpoint charges, which might not be the most cost-effective solution for such a large data volume.

C. VPC peering: This is the most cost-effective approach. VPC peering allows direct communication between VPCs without internet gateways or transit gateways, resulting in lower data transfer charges within the same AWS Region.

D. Transit Gateway with disabled cross-AZ: Disabling cross-AZ doesn't eliminate data transfer charges within the Region. It might only reduce traffic if services reside in different AZs than the NLB in the ingress VPC.

Here's why C is the best option:

It avoids transit gateway or PrivateLink charges for intra-region communication.

Using zonal NLB DNS names can minimize unnecessary cross-AZ traffic within the ingress VPC, potentially reducing data transfer costs within the AZ.

Additional cost optimization tips:

Consider using instance types with better price-performance for the services if compute costs are also a concern.

Explore Amazon EC2 Reserved Instances or Savings Plans for consistent workloads to potentially reduce compute costs.

Reference:

VPC peering offers the lowest overall cost when compared to other options for inter-VPC connectivity.

https://docs.aws.amazon.com/whitepapers/latest/building-scalable-secure-multi-vpc-network-infrastructure/vpc-to-vpc-connectivity.html

There is no such thing as "TG peering"; there are VPC peering and TG attachments.

43) Correct answer: B. Appliance mode is not enabled on the transit gateway attachment to the shared services VPC.

The issue lies with the configuration of the transit gateway attachment for the shared services VPC where the stateful appliances reside.

Let's analyze the options:

A. Separate subnet: While deploying the appliances and transit gateway attachments in separate subnets might introduce routing complexities, it wouldn't directly cause dropped traffic as long as proper routing rules are in place.

B. Appliance mode disabled (shared services VPC): This is the most likely culprit. Appliance mode on the transit gateway attachment in the shared services VPC ensures that traffic destined for the stateful appliances remains within the same Availability Zone for inspection and then routes back to the target VPC. Without appliance mode, the transit gateway might send packets to any available attachment (across AZs), potentially causing dropped packets if there's no corresponding route back in the source AZ.

C. Same subnet: Deploying both in the same subnet wouldn't inherently cause dropped traffic.

D. Appliance mode disabled (application VPCs): Appliance mode on the application VPC attachments is not relevant to the current issue of dropped traffic between VPCs. It affects traffic flow within an application VPC.

Therefore, the most probable reason for the dropped traffic is B. Appliance mode is not enabled on the transit gateway attachment to the shared services VPC. Enabling appliance mode on the shared services VPC attachment ensures traffic for inspection stays within the same AZ and avoids potential routing issues across AZs.

Reference:

If you read carefully the option says the stateful appliances and the transit gateway attachments are deployed in a "separate subnet". It does not mention anything about AZ. If you see the diagram following doc, then it is actually required that appliance and TGW attachment ENI should in different subnet, ow routing will not work.

https://docs.aws.amazon.com/vpc/latest/tgw/transit-gateway-appliance-scenario.html

44) Correct answer: C. Enable transit gateway appliance mode on the VPC attachment in the shared VPC.

The issue arises because the transit gateway might be sending traffic between VPCs (A and B) to random attachments across Availability Zones without proper routing guidance.

Let's analyze the options to identify the solution with the least management overhead:

A. VPN attachment and BGP: This introduces additional complexity with VPN tunnels, routing configurations, and BGP management, increasing overhead.

B. Appliance mode on VPC A and B attachments: While this might be necessary eventually, it's not directly relevant to the current issue. Appliance mode on application VPC attachments ensures traffic stays within the VPC for inspection by the firewall in the shared VPC.

C. Appliance mode on shared VPC attachment (BEST CHOICE): This is the most targeted solution with minimal additional management overhead. Enabling appliance mode on the transit gateway attachment in the shared VPC instructs the transit gateway to keep traffic for inspection within the same Availability Zone where the firewall resides. This ensures proper packet flow and avoids dropped traffic due to cross-AZ routing confusion.

D. VPC peering connections: VPC peering creates a direct connection between VPCs, bypassing the transit gateway. While it might work, it eliminates the central inspection point provided by the shared VPC with the firewall. Additionally, managing multiple VPC peering connections can be more complex than enabling a single setting (appliance mode) on the existing transit gateway attachment.

Therefore, enabling transit gateway appliance mode on the VPC attachment in the shared VPC (Option C) is the most efficient solution with minimal additional management overhead. It leverages the existing infrastructure and ensures traffic inspection by the firewall before routing to the destination VPC.

Reference:

https://docs.aws.amazon.com/vpc/latest/tgw/transit-gateway-appliance-scenario.html

the appliance mode must be enabled to keep the traffic in the same firewall appliance, regardless of the AZ where are the source and destination.

When appliance mode is not enabled, a transit gateway attempts to keep traffic routed between VPC attachments in the originating Availability Zone until it reaches its destination.

45) Correct answer: A. Configure an AWS Global Accelerator with an Application Load Balancer (ALB) endpoint. Attach the ALB to the Auto Scaling group. Configure an AWS WAF web ACL for the ALB to filter traffic based on the source IP address.

Here's the breakdown of the options to choose the solution that meets the requirements for gRPC traffic filtering based on source IP:

A. Global Accelerator with ALB and WAF: This is a strong contender. Global Accelerator can route traffic to the ALB, which supports gRPC and integrates well with WAF. WAF web ACLs can filter traffic based on source IP, addressing the security requirement.

B. Global Accelerator with NLB: NLBs operate at Layer 4 (TCP/UDP) and cannot handle gRPC, which requires Layer 7 functionalities.

C. CloudFront with ALB and WAF: CloudFront is a Content Delivery Network (CDN) not ideal for gRPC traffic, typically used for static content. However, ALB with WAF can achieve the filtering requirement.

D. CloudFront with NLB: Similar to B, NLB isn't suitable for gRPC.

Analysis:

While both A and C can achieve source IP filtering with WAF, CloudFront is not ideal for gRPC traffic.

Considering gRPC support and WAF integration, A. Global Accelerator with ALB and WAF is the most suitable solution.

Additional Note:

Security groups can also be used for basic IP filtering, but WAF web ACLs offer more granular control and rule-based filtering capabilities.

AWS Global Accelerator will deliver low-latency endpoints to the game's global user base. It will also route traffic over the AWS network backbone to the AWS Region hosting the game. The Application Load Balancer (ALB) will be configured to handle the gRPC protocol and preserve client IP addresses. It will distribute traffic to the Amazon EC2 instances in the Auto Scaling group to manage the game's load and will offer an endpoint compatible with the accelerator. To implement the required IP filtering, an AWS WAF web ACL will be associated with the ALB.

The other answer options do not meet the requirements. A Network Load Balancer does not support client IP

address preservation, and Amazon CloudFront does not support the gRPC protocol.

46) Correct answer: B. Create Amazon Route 53 private hosted zones and public hosted zones that have the same name, example.com. Associate the VPCs with the private hosted zone. Create records in each hosted zone that determine how traffic is routed.

The key requirement here is to achieve split-view DNS using Route 53 for the same domain name with different record sets for internal and external access to the website.

Let's analyze the options:

A. On-premises DNS server: This approach wouldn't leverage the split-view capabilities of Route 53. It would require manual configuration on each VPC's DHCP options, making it less scalable and secure.

B. Route 53 private and public hosted zones (BEST CHOICE): This is the recommended approach for split-view DNS with Route 53. By creating private and public hosted zones with the same domain name (example.com) and associating the VPCs with the private zone, Route 53 can direct internal DNS queries to the website's internal IP address within the VPC. Public queries will be resolved using the public hosted zone with the website's external IP address.

C. Route 53 Resolver with inbound/outbound endpoints: Route 53 Resolver provides DNS resolution services within a VPC. While it can be used for internal DNS resolution, it's not directly applicable to split-view DNS for a public website.

D. Route 53 Resolver with outbound/private zone: Similar to C, outbound endpoints and private hosted zones are used for internal DNS resolution within a VPC and wouldn't achieve split-view functionality for a public website.

Therefore, the most suitable solution is B. Create Amazon Route 53 private hosted zones and public hosted zones that have the same name, example.com. Associate the VPCs with the private hosted zone. Create records in each hosted zone that determine how traffic is routed. This approach leverages Route 53's built-in split-view capabilities for managing internal and external DNS records for the same domain name.

The solution requires split-view DNS, which is directly supported by Amazon Route 53. This can be achieved by creating public hosted zones and private hosted zones in Route 53 with the same name. If the private hosted zones are associated with VPCs, Route 53 Resolver will use the private hosted zones to answer queries from those VPCs and will use the public hosted zones to answer public queries.

The other options will not work. An on-premises DNS server cannot replace Route 53 Resolver for operations within the VPC. A Resolver inbound endpoint allows on-premises queries from on-premises networks to be resolved. A Resolver outbound endpoint is used to resolve queries from the VPC for on-premises addresses. However, neither of these Resolver endpoints will provide the necessary public and internal resolution.

47) Correct answer: C. Configure a Network Load Balancer (NLB) that includes a TCP listener on port 443. Create an Auto Scaling group for the EC2 instances. Configure the Auto Scaling group as the target group of the NLB. Configure TCP as the protocol for the target group

The application needs to scale to handle load and must use client certificates to authenticate directly with a web server. The solution requires that TLS sessions be connected to the underlying web server(s). To achieve this, an Auto Scaling group with a load balancer is needed. The load balancer must pass the TLS sessions to the Amazon EC2 instances. This architecture is supported by a Network Load Balancer (NLB) with a TCP listener on port 443. The NLB operates at the transport layer of the stack to pass the connection through to the web servers.

The other options would terminate the TLS connection from the client at the load balancer, which would prevent the client certificate from being visible to the web servers. Using an NLB with a TCP listener on port 443 is the only option that will maintain the session all the way from the client to the web servers in the Auto Scaling group.

48) The correct answer is:

B. Configure an S3 interface endpoint in the VPC. Configure the S3 interface endpoint DNS name in the on-premises application.

Explanation:

To allow the on-premises application to privately access the data stored in an S3 bucket created by the company, the network engineer should use an S3 interface endpoint (VPC endpoint) in the VPC. This allows traffic to flow securely between the on-premises data center and the S3 bucket over the AWS Direct Connect private Virtual Interface (VIF).

Option A is incorrect because an S3 gateway endpoint is used for accessing S3 from a VPC when using S3 as a gateway to another AWS service, such as AWS Glacier or S3 Transfer Acceleration.

Option C is incorrect because configuring an HTTP proxy on an Amazon EC2 instance introduces unnecessary complexity and is not the recommended approach for this scenario.

Option D is incorrect because configuring an HTTP proxy on an Amazon EC2 instance is not necessary when using an S3 interface endpoint for accessing S3 from a VPC.

The scenario calls for a solution enabling connectivity to Amazon S3 from both AWS workloads and an on-premises data center. An S3 interface endpoint can fulfill this requirement, allowing access from AWS workloads and supporting connections from the on-premises environment via AWS Direct Connect. To utilize the S3 interface endpoint, on-premises client applications must use the endpoint's DNS records.

Option A proposes a gateway endpoint, which relies on VPC route tables for routing and does not support DNS endpoint usage for on-premises applications. Option C, while potentially routing traffic, presents a single point of failure with an HTTP proxy server, failing to meet the high availability criteria. Option D also introduces an unnecessary single point of failure with an HTTP proxy and incorrectly suggests using an interface endpoint name in a route table.

49) The best solution for the network engineer to achieve traffic routing through the inspection VPC's firewalls is:

D. Enable transit gateway appliance mode for the VPC attachment to the inspection VPC.

Here's why this option is the most suitable:

Transit Gateway Appliance Mode: This feature forces traffic destined for other VPCs attached to the transit gateway to flow through the specific VPC attachment configured in appliance mode. In this case, enabling appliance mode for the inspection VPC attachment ensures all traffic between the application and backend VPCs is routed through the inspection VPC firewalls.

Stateful Firewalls: By design, stateful firewalls inspect traffic for security purposes, fulfilling the company's policy.

Let's explore why the other options are not ideal:

A. IPsec VPN connections: While VPNs can establish secure tunnels, they wouldn't force traffic routing through the inspection VPC. Traffic could potentially bypass the firewalls.

B. VRRP: VRRP is a redundancy protocol for routers, not ideal for enforcing traffic flow through a specific VPC for inspection.

C. BGP: BGP is a routing protocol for exchanging information between networks. While it can be used with transit gateway, it wouldn't guarantee all traffic flows through the inspection VPC firewalls.

Therefore, enabling transit gateway appliance mode offers a straightforward and effective solution to ensure traffic inspection compliance. The traffic will be directed through the inspection VPC, where the stateful firewalls can perform the necessary security checks.

The correct solution is to enable transit gateway appliance mode for the VPC attachment to the inspection VPC. The issue arises from cross-Availability Zone (AZ) traffic handling. Without appliance mode enabled, a transit gateway tries to keep traffic between VPC attachments within the originating AZ until it reaches its destination. This behavior causes return traffic to be routed to the virtual firewall in the firewall's local AZ instead of the AZ that initiated the traffic, leading to traffic drops.

Option A would create redundant connections and not provide the required symmetry for traffic to flow through the firewalls. Option B's mention of Virtual Router Redundancy Protocol (VRRP) for load sharing is not applicable because AWS does not support VRRP, which relies on multicast, a feature not supported within a VPC. Option C is incorrect because virtual firewall appliances cannot use Border Gateway Protocol (BGP) peering with a transit gateway.

50) The correct answer is: C. Recreate an asymmetric, customer managed key with an ECC_NIST_P256 key spec in the us-east-1 Region. Use this key to create a KSK.

Explanation:

Amazon Route 53 requires an asymmetric key with an ECC_NIST_P256 key spec for DNSSEC signing. Additionally, the key used for DNSSEC signing must be located in the us-east-1 Region. Therefore, the network engineer should create a new asymmetric customer-managed key with the ECC_NIST_P256 key spec in the us-east-1 Region and use this key to create the key-signing key (KSK) for DNSSEC signing in Route 53.

When Amazon Route 53 creates a key-signing key (KSK), it necessitates the use of a customer-managed key located in the us-east-1 Region. This key must be an asymmetric customer-managed key with an ECC_NIST_P256 key spec.

Option A is incorrect because it includes a symmetric key, which does not meet the requirement for an asymmetric key. Option D, although it includes an asymmetric key, is incorrect because it is in the wrong Region. Option B is incorrect because it uses the wrong key type and is also in the wrong Region. To create the KSK and support DNSSEC signing in Route 53, the key used must fulfill all these requirements.

51) The best configuration for BGP to achieve the desired traffic routing is:

A. Configure the local preference BGP community tag 7224:7300 for the transit VIF connected to Direct Connect connection 1.

Here's why this option meets the requirements:

Local Preference BGP Community Tag: This method influences the path selection during BGP route advertisement. A higher local preference value indicates a more preferred path.

Transit VIF 1 (us-east-1): Assigning a higher local preference (7224:7300) to the transit VIF connected to Direct Connect 1 (us-east-1) prioritizes traffic flow through this path.

Transit VIF 2 (us-west-2): The absence of a local preference tag on Transit VIF 2 (us-west-2) or a lower value would make it a secondary path.

Let's explore why the other options wouldn't achieve the desired outcome:

B. Local Preference (7224:9300) for Transit VIF 2: This would prioritize traffic through us-west-2 (opposite of the requirement).

C & D. Modifying AS_PATH: While AS_PATH reflects the path a route has taken, it doesn't directly influence preference based on the number of hops (prepend wouldn't achieve priority for us-east-1).

Therefore, using a higher local preference BGP community tag for the transit VIF connected to the primary data center (us-east-1) ensures traffic prioritization through that path. In case of failure, traffic would automatically failover to the secondary path (us-west-2) since it lacks a local preference tag or has a lower implicit value.

The correct approach is to configure the local BGP community tag 7224:7300 for the transit VIF connected to the first AWS Direct Connect connection. By default, AWS uses the distance from the local AWS Region to the Direct Connect location to determine the VIF or transit VIF for routing. However, you can modify this behavior by assigning local preference communities to VIFs. In this case, the goal is to give the VIF in Direct Connect connection 1 a higher preference.

Option B, which suggests using the 7224:9300 community tag, is incorrect. This tag is used to control how far a customer-advertised prefix is propagated and does not address the routing priority problem in this scenario. The other options propose using the AS_PATH attribute to control traffic between Direct Connect connections in multiple Regions, which is not suitable for handling multiple VIFs in this multi-Region environment.

52) The best solution to test the new application version with production traffic without impacting user experience is:

C. Implement Traffic Mirroring to replay the production requests to the test instances.

Here's why this option is ideal:

Traffic Mirroring: This feature allows capturing and replicating network traffic from a source (production instances) to a destination (test instances).

No User Impact: The original production traffic continues

serving users as usual. The mirrored traffic on the test instances doesn't interfere with production functionality.

Let's analyze why the other options might not be suitable:

A. Route 53 Weighted Routing: This option would potentially send some users to the new version, impacting their experience. It's not ideal for testing without user exposure.

B. ALB Weighted Target Groups: Similar to Route 53, weighted target groups within an ALB would distribute some traffic to the test instances, potentially affecting users.

D. NGINX Proxy Mirroring: While NGINX can mirror traffic, it would require additional configuration and management within the VPC, introducing complexity.

Traffic mirroring provides a safe and efficient method to test the new application version under realistic production traffic conditions without affecting user experience. The test instances receive a copy of the traffic, allowing developers to identify and address potential issues before a full deployment.

The correct solution is to use Traffic Mirroring. This method allows mirroring at the transport layer, capturing and mirroring all inbound requests into a test environment without affecting the performance of the production environment. It ensures that users do not encounter errors caused by testing the new version. The production environment continues to serve all user requests.

Other options would either expose some users to the new version of the application or add overhead and a potential failure point. These options would negatively impact the end user's experience by potentially exposing them to errors or performance problems.

53) The most cost-effective and suitable solution to address the DNS exfiltration vulnerability is:

B. Use Amazon Route 53 Resolver DNS Firewall. Configure a domain list with a rule group.

Here's why this option is the best fit:

Route 53 Resolver DNS Firewall: This managed service specifically addresses DNS filtering needs. It allows you to create rule groups with domain lists to block or allow DNS queries for specific domains.

Highly Available: Route 53 Resolver DNS Firewall is a managed service, eliminating the need to manage and maintain a separate DNS server like BIND. It's inherently highly available.

Cost-Effective: Compared to deploying and managing a dedicated filtering solution like BIND, Route 53 Resolver DNS Firewall offers a more cost-effective approach, especially for basic filtering needs.

Let's explore why the other options might not be ideal:

A. BIND Server with DNS filtering: While BIND can filter DNS requests, it requires additional configuration, maintenance, and wouldn't be inherently highly available without additional setup.

C. AWS Network Firewall with domain name filtering: This option offers broader security features but might be overkill for just DNS filtering. It can also be more complex to configure and manage, potentially increasing costs.

D. Route 53 Resolver Outbound Endpoint: While outbound endpoints can be used for routing DNS traffic, they don't offer the same level of built-in DNS filtering capabilities as Route 53

Resolver DNS Firewall.

Therefore, Route 53 Resolver DNS Firewall provides a managed, cost-effective, and highly available solution for the company to address the identified DNS exfiltration vulnerability.

Using Amazon Route 53 Resolver DNS Firewall, you can monitor and control the domains accessed by applications in your VPCs. DNS Firewall offers the use of allow lists or deny lists to filter the set of domains, effectively preventing DNS queries from being used to exfiltrate data.

While option A suggests configuring a BIND server with DNS filtering, this approach could work but would introduce a single point of failure. Additionally, managing a fleet of BIND servers with load balancers would be more complex and costly compared to the correct solution.

Option C mentions AWS Network Firewall, which can filter application and network layer traffic but lacks visibility into queries from Route 53 Resolver. Option D discusses configuring a Route 53 Resolver outbound endpoint, which forwards queries for specific domains to an on-premises DNS server but does not filter or block traffic.

54) The best solution to meet the new governance policy's logging requirements for DNS traffic is:

B. Configure Route 53 Resolver query logging for all VPCs. Send the logs to Amazon CloudWatch Logs. Use CloudWatch Logs Insights to query the IP address and DNS name.

Here's why this option effectively addresses the needs:

Route 53 Resolver Query Logging: This feature specifically captures logs for DNS queries resolved by Route 53 Resolver. Since the company already uses Route 53 Resolver for hybrid DNS, this is the most targeted approach.

CloudWatch Logs: Sending the logs to CloudWatch Logs provides a centralized and scalable solution for log storage and management.

CloudWatch Logs Insights: This service allows querying the CloudWatch logs to extract the desired information, including source IP address and requested DNS name, fulfilling the policy requirements.

Let's analyze why the other options are not as optimal:

A. VPC Flow Logs: VPC flow logs capture traffic information within a VPC, not specifically DNS queries. It wouldn't provide the granular details needed for DNS traffic analysis.

C. Site-to-Site VPN Logging: While logging VPN traffic might be possible, it wouldn't capture details within the AWS Cloud, as mandated by the policy.

D. Modifying Resolver Rules with S3 and Athena: Modifying existing rules to log to S3 would require additional configuration and wouldn't be as readily available for analysis as CloudWatch Logs. Athena can query S3 data, but it would involve separate steps for querying compared to CloudWatch Logs Insights.

Therefore, leveraging Route 53 Resolver query logging with CloudWatch Logs and CloudWatch Logs Insights offers a streamlined and efficient solution to meet the company's new DNS traffic logging policy requirements.

The correct approach is to configure Amazon Route 53 Resolver query logging for all VPCs, storing the logs in Amazon CloudWatch Logs for analysis using CloudWatch Logs Insights.

Option A, using flow logs, would not capture traffic from Amazon EC2 instances to the Amazon-provided DNS servers. Option C, AWS Site-to-Site VPN connections, does not provide an option for DNS logging. Option D, Route 53 Resolver rules, does not support logging configuration.

55) Correct answer: B. Configure the Amazon S3 bucket destination. Use Amazon Athena to determine which error messages the ALB is receiving.

Explanation:

After enabling access logging for the ALB, the next step is to configure the Amazon S3 bucket destination where the ALB access logs will be stored. Once the logs are stored in the S3 bucket, the network engineer can use Amazon Athena to query the logs and determine which error messages the ALB is receiving. Amazon Athena allows for interactive querying of data in S3 using standard SQL, making it suitable for analyzing log data.

ELB doesn't have direct integration with CloudWatch. ELB can drop the logs in S3 bucket and Athena can be used to analyze the logs.

Reference:

Access logs is an optional feature of Elastic Load Balancing that is disabled by default. After you enable access logs for your load balancer, Elastic Load Balancing captures the logs and stores them in the Amazon S3 bucket that you specify as compressed files. You can disable access logs at any time.

https://docs.aws.amazon.com/elasticloadbalancing/latest/
application/load-balancer-access-logs.html

56) Correct answer: C. Place the EC2 instances in a private subnet. Create an interface VPC endpoint for Amazon SQS. Create gateway VPC endpoints for Amazon S3 and DynamoDB.

Explanation:

This solution ensures that the EC2 instances do not have public IP addresses, meeting the company's requirement. Placing the instances in a private subnet provides an additional layer of security. Using interface VPC endpoints for Amazon S3 and DynamoDB allows the EC2 instances to access these services without traversing the internet, improving security and reducing costs. Finally, creating a gateway VPC endpoint for Amazon SQS enables the EC2 instances to access the SQS queue without needing public IP addresses or internet access.

References:

Interface endpoint:

https://docs.aws.amazon.com/vpc/latest/privatelink/aws-
services-privatelink-support.html

Gateway not supported service:

https://docs.aws.amazon.com/vpc/latest/privatelink/gateway-
endpoints.html

57) To meet the requirements for a hybrid DNS solution that integrates application-specific hostnames with centrally

managed DNS hostnames from the on-premises network and provides bidirectional name resolution while minimizing management overhead, the network engineer should take the following steps:

A. Use an Amazon Route 53 Resolver inbound endpoint: This allows DNS queries from the on-premises network to resolve AWS-hosted DNS names by forwarding those queries to the Amazon Route 53 Resolver.

C. Use an Amazon Route 53 Resolver outbound endpoint: This enables DNS queries from within the AWS environment to be forwarded to the on-premises DNS server, allowing resolution of on-premises DNS names.

E. Create Amazon Route 53 private hosted zones: This allows individual teams to manage their own DNS hostnames for their applications within their development environment, while integrating with the overall DNS infrastructure.

Explanation:

Inbound Endpoint (A): Facilitates DNS queries originating from the on-premises network to resolve DNS names hosted in AWS, which is essential for bidirectional name resolution.

Outbound Endpoint (C): Enables DNS queries from the AWS environment to be forwarded to the on-premises DNS servers, completing the bidirectional DNS query capability.

Private Hosted Zones (E): Allows individual teams to manage DNS hostnames for their applications within AWS, integrating these with the on-premises DNS setup, and reduces the management overhead by leveraging AWS-managed DNS services.

The other options are less suitable because:

B. Modify the DHCP options set by setting a custom DNS server value: While this can help point instances to a custom DNS server, it doesn't integrate the AWS and on-premises DNS zones as effectively as Route 53 Resolver endpoints.

D. Create DNS proxy servers: This introduces additional management overhead and complexity, which the requirement aims to minimize.

F. Set up a zone transfer between Amazon Route 53 and the on-premises DNS: Route 53 does not support zone transfers, making this option infeasible.

Thus, the best steps to take are A, C, and E.

For bidirectional name resolution, both Route 53 Resolver inbound & outbound endpoint is required.

Reference:

https://aws.amazon.com/blogs/networking-and-content-delivery/centralized-dns-management-of-hybrid-cloud-with-amazon-route-53-and-aws-transit-gateway/

58) The most cost-effective and efficient solution to identify the AWS resources generating suspicious traffic while minimizing administrative overhead is:

C. Use VPC flow logs. Publish the flow logs to a log group in Amazon CloudWatch Logs. Use CloudWatch Logs Insights to query the flow logs to identify the AWS resources.

Here's why this option meets the requirements:

VPC Flow Logs: VPC flow logs are readily available and capture network traffic information within the VPC. They provide details like source and destination IP addresses, ports, and bytes transferred.

CloudWatch Logs: Sending the flow logs to CloudWatch Logs offers a centralized and scalable solution for log storage and analysis.

CloudWatch Logs Insights: This serverless service allows querying the CloudWatch logs to filter and analyze the flow logs. You can search for specific destination IP addresses from the deny list and identify the source ENIs (Elastic Network Interfaces) associated with the suspicious traffic. This information can then be used to pinpoint the AWS resources (EC2 instances, Lambda functions, etc.) attached to those ENIs.

This approach is cost-effective because it utilizes existing managed services offered by AWS. CloudWatch Logs offers a free tier for log ingestion and storage up to a certain limit, making it suitable for smaller investigations. CloudWatch Logs Insights pricing is based on the amount of data scanned during queries.

Let's explore why the other options are less ideal:

A. Launching an EC2 Instance with Traffic Mirroring: This approach incurs additional costs for launching and managing an EC2 instance. Analyzing captured traffic with open-source tools introduces further complexity and potential licensing costs.

B. SIEM Solution in VPC: While SIEM solutions offer advanced security capabilities, deploying and managing a SIEM solution within the VPC would be more resource-intensive and expensive compared to CloudWatch Logs.

D. Kinesis Data Stream and Athena: This option involves multiple services (Kinesis Data Stream, Kinesis Data Firehose, S3, and Athena) and requires additional configuration and management overhead. Athena pricing is based on data scanned per query, and S3 storage costs can accumulate over time.

Therefore, leveraging VPC flow logs with CloudWatch Logs and CloudWatch Logs Insights provides a cost-effective and efficient way to identify the AWS resources generating suspicious traffic while minimizing administrative overhead.

59) The correct answer is A. Use a Network Load Balancer to automatically preserve the source IP address.

Explanation:

Option A: A Network Load Balancer (NLB) is designed to handle TCP/UDP traffic and automatically preserves the source IP address of the clients, which is a requirement in this scenario.

Option B: The X-Forwarded-For header is used by Application Load Balancers (ALBs) for HTTP/HTTPS traffic to capture the original IP address of the client. This option is not applicable for Network Load Balancers.

Option C: Enabling the ProxyProtocol v2 attribute on an NLB can also preserve the source IP address and provide additional metadata. However, this might not be necessary if automatic preservation by the NLB itself suffices.

Option D: Application Load Balancers use the X-Forwarded-For header to preserve the client's IP address but are not suitable for non-web (TCP/UDP) applications.

Therefore, using a Network Load Balancer is the most straightforward and appropriate solution to ensure that the source IP addresses are preserved and passed through to the on-premises servers.

60) A and E are the correct steps to achieve the desired configuration.

Explanation:

A. Insert a Rule for the Load Balancer HTTPS Listener: This step ensures that requests with the /management path prefix from the on-premises IP address space are correctly routed to the management application target group. Enabling stickiness in the management application target group ensures that session data is preserved if required.

E. Forward All Requests to the Web Application Target Group: By forwarding all other requests to the web application target group and disabling stickiness, the default traffic (non-management requests) will be handled correctly without session stickiness, which is suitable for a stateless web application.

Incorrect Options:

B: Modifying the default rule incorrectly affects the routing logic for non-management traffic.

C: Checking the X-Forwarded-For header is less reliable than using the source-ip condition.

D: Forwarding requests based on a negative match for the /management prefix can lead to routing errors.

By following steps A and E, the network engineer ensures that both the web and management applications are correctly routed based on the specified conditions while maintaining the required security and access controls.

Reference:

DEFAULT RULES CANNOT HAVE CONDITIONS so B & D are out.

A to forward people to managment with stickiness

E to forward people to the web application without stickiness

https://docs.aws.amazon.com/elasticloadbalancing/latest/application/load-balancer-listeners.html

Also see:

https://docs.aws.amazon.com/elasticloadbalancing/latest/application/listener-update-rules.html#edit-rule

Step 8 - "(Optional) Modify the conditions and actions as needed. For example, you can edit a condition or action (pencil icon), add a condition, add an authenticate action to a rule for an HTTPS listener, or delete a condition or action (trash can icon). You can't add conditions to the default rule."

61) The correct answer is: C. Create VPC flow logs in a custom format. Set the application subnets as resources. Include the pkt-srcaddr field and the pkt-dstaddr field in the flow logs.

Explanation:

Option A: Creating VPC flow logs in the default format and filtering for EKS nodes will not provide the specific packet-level details (pkt-srcaddr and pkt-dstaddr) needed to identify POD IP addresses.

Option B: While creating VPC flow logs in a custom format and setting the EKS nodes as the resource, it will provide specific information about the source and destination IP addresses of the packets from EKS nodes. However, it might miss some relevant traffic if it's not exclusively from the nodes themselves.

Option C: This option involves creating VPC flow logs in a custom format, setting the application subnets as resources, and including the pkt-srcaddr and pkt-dstaddr fields. This approach ensures that all traffic within the application subnets is captured with the necessary details about source and destination IP addresses. By focusing on the application subnets, it captures all relevant traffic, including communication between PODs and services.

Option D: Creating VPC flow logs in a custom format and filtering for EKS nodes with the pkt-srcaddr and pkt-dstaddr fields might miss some traffic that doesn't directly involve the nodes but is still within the application subnets.

Thus, Option C is the most comprehensive and ensures that the security team can monitor all relevant traffic within the specified subnets with minimal operational overhead.

References:

https://docs.aws.amazon.com/cli/latest/reference/ec2/create-flow-logs.html

You cannot set the EKS nodes as the resource of a VPC flow log. So, B is wrong.

C and D are correct.

But "The security team wants to limit the number of flows logs and wants to examine the traffic from only the two applications".

So, it is easier to set the resource of the VPC flow logs to the subnets of the two clusters.

So, answer is C.

You can only use Ips:

https://aws.amazon.com/blogs/networking-and-content-delivery/using-vpc-flow-logs-to-capture-and-query-eks-network-communications/

62) The most suitable solution for the IoT company to migrate its MQTT infrastructure to AWS and minimize latency for globally distributed sensor modules involves:

B. Place the EC2 instances behind a Network Load Balancer (NLB). Configure TCP listeners. Create an AWS Global Accelerator in front of the NLB. Use Bring Your Own IP (BYOIP) from the on-premises network with Global Accelerator.

Here's why this approach effectively addresses the needs:

EC2 Instances with NLB: Since MQTT is a lightweight messaging protocol primarily utilizing TCP connections, an NLB is well-suited for high-throughput, low-latency traffic distribution. Configuring TCP listeners ensures proper handling of MQTT communication.

AWS Global Accelerator: This service routes traffic from the globally distributed sensor modules to the optimal AWS region where the NLB resides. This significantly reduces latency compared to direct connections to the on-premises brokers.

BYOIP with Global Accelerator: By assigning a public IP address from the company's on-premises network to the Global Accelerator, the sensor modules with hardcoded public IPs can continue communicating with the MQTT brokers without reconfiguration. This minimizes the disruption to existing deployments.

Let's analyze why the other options are not ideal:

A. NLB with BYOIP only: While NLB and BYOIP address part of the requirement, they wouldn't improve latency for globally distributed sensor modules.

C. ALB with Global Accelerator: While ALB supports TCP

listeners, it's typically used for HTTP/HTTPS traffic. An NLB is more efficient for this scenario.

D. CloudFront with BYOIP: CloudFront is a content delivery network (CDN) optimized for static content delivery. It's not suitable for real-time data streaming like MQTT.

Therefore, using an NLB with BYOIP behind a Global Accelerator offers a scalable and low-latency solution for the company's MQTT infrastructure migration while minimizing the need to reconfigure existing sensor modules.

Reference:

Global accelerator + NLB

https://aws.amazon.com/blogs/iot/creating-static-ip-addresses-and-custom-domains-for-aws-iot-core-endpoints/

63) The most scalable approach to add VPCs with on-premises connectivity when reaching the limit for VPCs and private VIFs per AWS Direct Connect connection is:

D. Create a transit gateway, and attach the VPCs. Create a Direct Connect gateway, and associate it with the transit gateway. Create a transit VIF to the Direct Connect gateway.

Here's why this option offers the best scalability:

Transit Gateway: This service acts as a central hub for routing traffic between VPCs and on-premises networks. By attaching all VPCs that need on-premises connectivity to the transit gateway, you eliminate the limitation of private VIFs per Direct Connect connection.

Direct Connect Gateway: This gateway connects the transit gateway to the AWS Direct Connect link. Traffic from the VPCs can then flow through the transit gateway and out to the on-premises network via Direct Connect.

Transit VIF: This virtual interface connects the transit gateway to the Direct Connect gateway, providing the actual connection to the on-premises network.

Let's explore why the other options are less scalable:

A. New Direct Connect Connection: While this would provide additional VIFs initially, it wouldn't be scalable in the long run as the company keeps adding VPCs.

B. Virtual Private Gateways with VPN: Site-to-Site VPN connections are not as reliable or performant as Direct Connect for high-bandwidth traffic. Additionally, managing multiple VPN connections can become cumbersome as the number of VPCs grows.

C. Direct Connect Gateway with VPC Associations: This option allows associating more VPCs than the single VIF limit, but it doesn't provide the centralized routing and scalability benefits of a transit gateway.

Therefore, using a transit gateway with a Direct Connect gateway offers a scalable and centrally managed solution for connecting numerous VPCs with on-premises connectivity when AWS Direct Connect limitations are reached.

Using DXGW with TGW allow you to also be flexible in case of expanding to new regions with more TGW in those regions.

64) Correct answer: AC

A. The EC2 instance is not attached to an IAM role that allows write operations to Amazon SQS.

C. There is no interface VPC endpoint configured for Amazon SQS.

A - EC2 requires IAM role that allows write operations to Amazon SQS.

C - Being in private subnet, interface endpoint is required to access SQS.

B. Incorrect, default SG allows 0.0.0.0/0 on any port for outbound traffic from EC2

D. Incorrect, Network ACL allows 0.0.0.0/0 inbound by default

E. Incorrect, Amazon SQS uses interface endpoint (privatelink), so no routes are needed in the routing table unlike Gateway Endpoints.

References:

See Note at the top of page. https://docs.aws.amazon.com/AWSSimpleQueueService/latest/SQSDeveloperGuide/sqs-basic-examples-of-iam-policies.html

https://docs.aws.amazon.com/AWSSimpleQueueService/latest/SQSDeveloperGuide/sqs-sending-messages-from-vpc.html

65) The minimum requirements for your router to enable the use of your first virtual interface with a 1-Gbps AWS Direct Connect connection are:

B. 1-Gbps Single Mode Fiber Interface, 802.1Q VLAN, Peer IP Address, BGP Session with MD5.

Here's why these components are essential:

1-Gbps Single Mode Fiber Interface: AWS Direct Connect uses single-mode fiber optic cables for high-bandwidth, low-loss data transmission.

802.1Q VLAN (Virtual LAN): This allows tagging traffic for the Direct Connect connection within your network, separating it from other traffic.

Peer IP Address: This is a public IP address assigned to your router's interface by AWS for the Direct Connect connection. It will be used for communication with AWS.

BGP Session with MD5: Border Gateway Protocol (BGP) is the dynamic routing protocol used by AWS Direct Connect to exchange routing information. MD5 authentication provides basic security for the BGP session.

Let's explore why the other options are not minimal requirements:

A. Multi-Mode Fiber: While multi-mode fiber can be used for shorter distances, single-mode fiber is the standard for AWS Direct Connect connections due to its superior performance over long distances.

C. IPsec Parameters: IPsec encryption is an optional security layer that can be added on top of BGP, but it's not a minimum requirement.

D. Route-Map, Prefix List, GRE Tunnel: These are advanced routing configurations that might be used for specific scenarios but are not essential for basic functionality.

Therefore, with a single-mode fiber interface, VLAN tagging, a peer IP address, and a BGP session with MD5 authentication, your router can establish the minimum connection required to utilize your first virtual interface with AWS Direct Connect.

PRACTICE TEST II

1) A data analytics company operates a 100-node high-performance computing (HPC) cluster for parallel data processing within a VPC in the AWS Cloud. As part of its workflow, the HPC cluster needs to perform numerous DNS queries to connect to Amazon RDS databases, Amazon S3 buckets, and on-premises data stores accessible via AWS Direct Connect. During peak events at the end of the year, the HPC cluster can scale up by five to seven times.

The company currently uses two Amazon EC2 instances as the primary DNS servers for the VPC. These instances are configured to forward queries to the default VPC resolver for Amazon Route 53 hosted domains and to on-premises DNS servers for other on-premises hosted domain names. The company has observed job failures and determined that DNS queries from the HPC cluster nodes fail when attempting to resolve RDS and S3 bucket endpoints.

Which architectural change should a network engineer implement to provide the DNS service in the MOST scalable way?

A. Scale out the DNS service by adding two additional EC2 instances in the VPC. Reconfigure half of the HPC cluster nodes to use these new DNS servers. Plan to scale out by adding additional EC2 instance-based DNS servers in the future as the HPC cluster size grows.

B. Scale up the existing EC2 instances that the company is using as DNS servers. Change the instance size to the largest possible instance size to accommodate the current DNS load and the anticipated load in the future.

C. Create Route 53 Resolver outbound endpoints. Create Route 53 Resolver rules to forward queries to on-premises DNS servers for on premises hosted domain names. Reconfigure the HPC cluster nodes to use the default VPC resolver instead of the EC2 instance-based DNS servers. Terminate the EC2 instances.

D. Create Route 53 Resolver inbound endpoints. Create rules on the on-premises DNS servers to forward queries to the default VPC resolver. Reconfigure the HPC cluster nodes to forward all DNS queries to the on-premises DNS servers. Terminate the EC2 instances.

2) A company's network engineer is designing an active-passive connection to AWS from two on-premises data centers. AWS Direct Connect connections are established between the on-premises data centers and AWS. Each location uses a transit virtual interface (VIF) that connects to a Direct Connect gateway, which is associated with a transit gateway.

The network engineer must ensure that traffic from AWS is primarily routed to the primary data center, with routing to the failover data center occurring only in the event of an outage.

Which solution will meet these requirements?

A. Set the BGP community tag for all prefixes from the primary data center to 7224:7100. Set the BGP community tag for all prefixes from the failover data center to 7224:7300

B. Set the BGP community tag for all prefixes from the primary data center to 7224:7300. Set the BGP community tag for all prefixes from the failover data center to 7224:7100

C. Set the BGP community tag for all prefixes from the primary data center to 7224:9300. Set the BGP community tag for all prefixes from the failover data center to 7224:9100

D. Set the BGP community tag for all prefixes from the primary data center to 7224:9100. Set the BGP community tag for all prefixes from the failover data center to 7224:9300

3) A real estate company utilizes Amazon Workspaces to provide corporate-managed desktop services to its agents globally. These Workspaces are deployed across seven VPCs, each located in a different AWS Region.

Due to a new requirement, the company's cloud-hosted security information and event management (SIEM) system needs to analyze DNS queries generated by the Workspaces to identify the target domains they are connecting to. The SIEM system supports both poll and push methods for data and log collection.

Which solution should a network engineer implement to meet these requirements MOST cost-effectively?

A. Create VPC flow logs in each VPC that is connected to the Workspaces instances. Publish the log data to a central Amazon S3 bucket. Configure the SIEM system to poll the S3 bucket periodically.

B. Configure an Amazon CloudWatch agent to log all DNS requests in Amazon CloudWatch Logs. Configure a subscription filter in CloudWatch Logs. Push the logs to the SIEM system by using Amazon Kinesis Data Firehose.

C. Configure VPC Traffic Mirroring to copy network traffic from each Workspace and to send the traffic to the SIEM system probes for analysis.

D. Configure Amazon Route 53 query logging. Set the destination as an Amazon Kinesis Data Firehose delivery stream that is configured to push data to the SIEM system.

4) A company has an AWS Direct Connect connection between its on-premises data center in the United States (US) and its workloads in the us-east-1 Region. This connection utilizes a transit virtual interface (VIF) to link the data center to a transit gateway in us-east-1.

The company is opening a new office in Europe, including a new on-premises data center in England. A Direct Connect connection will link this new data center to workloads running in a single VPC in the eu-west-2 Region. The company needs to establish connectivity between the US data center and us-east-1 with the Europe data center and eu-west-2. A network engineer must ensure full connectivity between the data centers and Regions, aiming for the lowest possible latency.

How should the network engineer design the network architecture to meet these requirements?

A. Connect the VPC in eu-west-2 with the Europe data center by using a Direct Connect gateway and a private VIF. Associate the transit gateway in us-east-1 with the same Direct Connect gateway. Enable SiteLink for the transit VIF and the private VIF.

B. Connect the VPC in eu-west-2 to a new transit gateway. Connect the Europe data center to the new transit gateway by using a Direct Connect gateway and a new transit VIF. Associate the transit gateway in us-east-1 with the same Direct Connect gateway. Enable SiteLink for both transit VIFs. Peer the two transit gateways.

C. Connect the VPC in eu-west-2 to a new transit gateway.

Connect the Europe data center to the new transit gateway by using a Direct Connect gateway and a new transit VIF. Create a new Direct Connect gateway. Associate the transit gateway in us-east-1 with the new Direct Connect gateway. Enable SiteLink for both transit VIFs. Peer the two transit gateways.

D. Connect the VPC in eu-west-2 with the Europe data center by using a Direct Connect gateway and a private VIF. Create a new Direct Connect gateway. Associate the transit gateway in us-east-1 with the new Direct Connect gateway. Enable SiteLink for the transit VIF and the private VIF.

5) A network engineer needs to standardize the company's approach to centralizing and managing interface VPC endpoints for private communication with AWS services. The company utilizes AWS Transit Gateway for inter-VPC connectivity between AWS accounts in a hub-and-spoke model. The network services team is responsible for managing all Amazon Route 53 zones and interface endpoints within a shared services AWS account. The company wants to use this centralized model to allow AWS resources to access AWS Key Management Service (AWS KMS) without routing traffic over the public internet.

What should the network engineer do to meet these requirements?

A. In the shared services account, create an interface endpoint for AWS KMS. Modify the interface endpoint by disabling the private DNS name. Create a private hosted zone in the shared services account with an alias record that points to the interface endpoint. Associate the private hosted zone with the spoke VPCs in each AWS account.

B. In the shared services account, create an interface endpoint for AWS KMS. Modify the interface endpoint by disabling the private DNS name. Create a private hosted zone in each spoke AWS account with an alias record that points to the interface endpoint. Associate each private hosted zone with the shared services AWS account.

C. In each spoke AWS account, create an interface endpoint for AWS KMS. Modify each interface endpoint by disabling the private DNS name. Create a private hosted zone in each spoke AWS account with an alias record that points to each interface endpoint. Associate each private hosted zone with the shared services AWS account.

D. In each spoke AWS account, create an interface endpoint for AWS KMS. Modify each interface endpoint by disabling the private DNS name. Create a private hosted zone in the shared services account with an alias record that points to each interface endpoint. Associate the private hosted zone with the spoke VPCs in each AWS account.

6) A company has deployed its AWS environment in a single AWS Region, consisting of several hundred application VPCs, a shared services VPC, and a VPN connection to the company's on-premises environment. A network engineer needs to implement a transit gateway with the following requirements:

- **Application VPCs must be isolated from each other.**
- **Bidirectional communication must be allowed between the application VPCs and the on-premises network.**
- **Bidirectional communication must be allowed between the application VPCs and the shared services VPC.**

The network engineer creates the transit gateway with default route table association and default route table propagation options disabled. Additionally, the network engineer creates a VPN attachment for the on-premises network and VPC attachments for the application VPCs and the shared services VPC.

To meet all the requirements with the minimum number of transit gateway route tables, the network engineer must design an appropriate solution.

Which combination of actions should the network engineer perform to accomplish this goal? (Choose two.)

A. Configure a separate transit gateway route table for on premises. Associate the VPN attachment with this transit gateway route table. Propagate all application VPC attachments to this transit gateway route table.

B. Configure a separate transit gateway route table for each application VPC. Associate each application VPC attachment with its respective transit gateway route table. Propagate the shared services VPC attachment and the VPN attachment to this transit gateway route table.

C. Configure a separate transit gateway route table for all application VPCs. Associate all application VPCs with this transit gateway route table. Propagate the shared services VPC attachment and the VPN attachment to this transit gateway route table.

D. Configure a separate transit gateway route table for the shared services VPC. Associate the shared services VPC attachment with this transit gateway route table. Propagate all application VPC attachments to this transit gateway route table.

E. Configure a separate transit gateway route table for on premises and the shared services VPC. Associate the VPN attachment and the shared services VPC attachment with this transit gateway route table. Propagate all application VPC attachments to this transit gateway route table.

7) A company has created three VPCs: a production VPC, a nonproduction VPC, and a shared services VPC. The production VPC and the nonproduction VPC must each be able to communicate with the shared services VPC. However, there must be no communication between the production VPC and the nonproduction VPC. A transit gateway is deployed to enable communication between the VPCs.

Which route table configurations on the transit gateway will meet these requirements?

A. Configure a route table with the production and nonproduction VPC attachments associated with propagated routes for only the shared services VPC. Create an additional route table with only the shared services VPC attachment associated with propagated routes from the production and nonproduction VPCs.

B. Configure a route table with the production and nonproduction VPC attachments associated with propagated routes for each VPC. Create an additional route table with only the shared services VPC attachment associated with propagated routes from each VPC.

C. Configure a route table with all the VPC attachments associated with propagated routes for only the shared services VPCreate an additional route table with only the shared services VPC attachment associated with propagated routes from the production and nonproduction VPCs.

D. Configure a route table with the production and nonproduction VPC attachments associated with propagated routes disabled. Create an additional route table with only the shared services VPC attachment associated with propagated routes from the production and nonproduction VPCs.

8) A company is utilizing an AWS Site-to-Site VPN connection from its on-premises data center to a virtual private gateway in the AWS Cloud. Due to congestion, the company is encountering availability and performance issues as traffic traverses the internet before reaching AWS. A network engineer needs to swiftly mitigate these issues for the connection with minimal administrative effort.

Which solution will meet these requirements?

A. Edit the existing Site-to-Site VPN connection by enabling acceleration. Stop and start the VPN service on the customer gateway for the new setting to take effect.

B. Configure a transit gateway in the same AWS Region as the existing virtual private gateway. Create a new accelerated Site-to-Site VPN connection. Connect the new connection to the transit gateway by using a VPN attachment. Update the customer gateway device to use the new Site to Site VPN connection. Delete the existing Site-to-Site VPN connection

C. Create a new accelerated Site-to-Site VPN connection. Connect the new Site-to-Site VPN connection to the existing virtual private gateway. Update the customer gateway device to use the new Site-to-Site VPN connection. Delete the existing Site-to-Site VPN connection.

D. Create a new AWS Direct Connect connection with a private VIF between the on-premises data center and the AWS Cloud. Update the customer gateway device to use the new Direct Connect connection. Delete the existing Site-to-Site VPN connection.

9) An Australian ecommerce company hosts all of its services in the AWS Cloud and is looking to expand its customer base

to the United States (US), specifically targeting the western US for expansion.

The company's current AWS architecture includes four AWS accounts with multiple VPCs deployed in the ap-southeast-2 Region. All VPCs are connected to a transit gateway in ap-southeast-2, with dedicated VPCs for each application service and additional VPCs for centralized security features such as proxies, firewalls, and logging.

To expand into the US, the company plans to replicate its infrastructure from ap-southeast-2 to the us-west-1 Region. A network engineer needs to establish connectivity between the various applications in the two Regions, aiming to maximize bandwidth, minimize latency, and reduce operational overhead.

Which solution will meet these requirements?

A. Create VPN attachments between the two transit gateways. Configure the VPN attachments to use BGP routing between the two transit gateways.

B. Peer the transit gateways in each Region. Configure routing between the two transit gateways for each Region's IP addresses.

C. Create a VPN server in a VPC in each Region. Update the routing to point to the VPN servers for the IP addresses in alternate Regions.

D. Attach the VPCs in us-west-1 to the transit gateway in ap-southeast-2.

10) A company is utilizing Amazon Route 53 Resolver DNS Firewall within a VPC to block all domains except those on an approved list. Concerned about potential impact, the company worries that if DNS Firewall becomes unresponsive, it could

affect VPC resources by preventing DNS query resolution. To uphold application service level agreements, the company requires DNS queries to resolve even in scenarios where Route 53 Resolver does not receive a response from DNS Firewall.

Which change should a network engineer implement to meet these requirements?

A. Update the DNS Firewall VPC configuration to disable fail open for the VPC.

B. Update the DNS Firewall VPC configuration to enable fail open for the VPC.

C. Create a new DHCP options set with parameter dns_firewall_fail_open=false. Associate the new DHCP options set with the VPC.

D. Create a new DHCP options set with parameter dns_firewall_fail_open=true. Associate the new DHCP options set with the VPC.

11) A financial company located in the us-east-1 Region needs to establish secure connectivity to AWS. The company has two on-premises data centers, both located within the same Region. The network team must establish hybrid connectivity to the AWS environment, ensuring reliable and consistent connectivity.

The connection should provide access to the company's private resources within its AWS environment, which are located in the us-east-1 and us-west-2 Regions. It should also allow corporate network resources to send large amounts of data to Amazon S3 over the same connection. To comply with regulations, the connection must be highly available and encrypt all packets sent between the on-premises location and any AWS services.

Which combination of steps should the network team take to meet these requirements? (Choose two.)

A. Set up a private VIF to send data to Amazon S3. Use an AWS Site-to-Site VPN connection over the private VIF to encrypt data in transit to the VPCs in us-east-1 and us-west-2.

B. Set up an AWS Direct Connect connection to each of the company's data centers.

C. Set up an AWS Direct Connect connection from one of the company's data centers to us-east-1 and us-west-2.

D. Set up a public VIF to send data to Amazon S3. Use an AWS Site-to-Site VPN connection over the public VIF to encrypt data in transit to the VPCs in us-east-1 and us-west-2.

E. Set up a transit VIF for an AWS Direct Connect gateway to send data to Amazon S3. Create a transit gateway. Associate the transit gateway with the Direct Connect gateway to provide secure communications from the company's data centers to the VPCs in us-east-1 and us-west-2.

12) A company intends to utilize Amazon S3 to archive financial data currently housed in an on-premises data center. The company employs AWS Direct Connect with a Direct Connect gateway and a transit gateway for connectivity to the on-premises data center. Transporting the data over the public internet is prohibited, necessitating encryption of the data in transit.

Which solution will meet these requirements?

A. Create a Direct Connect public VIF. Set up an IPsec VPN connection over the public VIF to access Amazon S3. Use HTTPS for communication.

B. Create an IPsec VPN connection over the transit VIF. Create a VPC and attach the VPC to the transit gateway. In the VPC, provision an interface VPC endpoint for Amazon S3. Use HTTPS for communication.

C. Create a VPC and attach the VPC to the transit gateway. In the VPC, provision an interface VPC endpoint for Amazon S3. Use HTTPS for communication.

D. Create a Direct Connect public VIF. Set up an IPsec VPN connection over the public VIF to the transit gateway. Create an attachment for Amazon S3. Use HTTPS for communication.

13) A company hosts a web application on Amazon EC2 instances behind an Application Load Balancer (ALB), which serves as the origin for an Amazon CloudFront distribution. The company seeks to implement a custom authentication system to issue tokens for authenticated customers.

The web application must verify that GET/POST requests originate from authenticated customers before delivering the content. A network engineer needs to design a solution that enables the web application to identify authorized customers.

What is the MOST operationally efficient solution that meets these requirements?

A. Use the ALB to inspect the authorized token inside the GET/POST request payload. Use an AWS Lambda function to insert a customized header to inform the web application of an authenticated customer request.

B. Integrate AWS WAF with the ALB to inspect the authorized token inside the GET/POST request payload. Configure the ALB listener to insert a customized header to inform the web application of an authenticated customer request.

C. Use an AWS Lambda@Edge function to inspect the authorized token inside the GET/POST request payload. Use the Lambda@Edge function also to insert a customized header to inform the web application of an authenticated customer request.

D. Set up an EC2 instance that has a third-party packet inspection tool to inspect the authorized token inside the GET/POST request payload. Configure the tool to insert a customized header to inform the web application of an authenticated customer request.

14) A company has its production VPC (VPC-A) in the eu-west-1 Region in Account 1. VPC-A is connected to a transit gateway (TGW-A), which is in turn linked to an on-premises data center in Dublin, Ireland, via an AWS Direct Connect transit VIF configured for an AWS Direct Connect gateway. Additionally, the company has a staging VPC (VPC-B) attached to another transit gateway (TGW-B) in the eu-west-2 Region in Account 2.

A network engineer needs to establish connectivity between VPC-B and the on-premises data center in Dublin.

Which solutions will meet these requirements? (Choose two.)

A. Configure inter-Region VPC peering between VPC-A and VPC-B. Add the required VPC peering routes. Add the VPC-B CIDR block in the allowed prefixes on the Direct Connect gateway association.

B. Associate TGW-B with the Direct Connect gateway. Advertise the VPC-B CIDR block under the allowed prefixes.

C. Configure another transit VIF on the Direct Connect connection and associate TGW-B. Advertise the VPC-B CIDR block under the allowed prefixes.

D. Configure inter-Region transit gateway peering between TGW-A and TGW-B. Add the peering routes in the transit gateway route tables. Add both the VPC-A and the VPC-B CIDR block under the allowed prefix list in the Direct Connect gateway association.

E. Configure an AWS Site-to-Site VPN connection over the transit VIF to TGW-B as a VPN attachment.

15) A network engineer is planning a hybrid architecture that involves a 1 Gbps AWS Direct Connect connection between the company's data center and two AWS Regions: us-east-1 and eu-west-1. The VPCs in us-east-1 are linked via a transit gateway and require access to multiple on-premises databases. Per company policy, only one VPC in eu-west-1 can connect to a specific on-premises server. The on-premises network manages traffic segmentation between the databases and the server.

How should the network engineer set up the Direct Connect connection to meet these requirements?

A. Create one hosted connection. Use a transit VIF to connect to the transit gateway in us-east-1. Use a private VIF to connect to the VPC in eu-west-1. Use one Direct. Connect gateway for both VIFs to route from the Direct Connect locations to the corresponding AWS Region along the path that has the lowest latency.

B. Create one hosted connection. Use a transit VIF to connect to the transit gateway in us-east-1. Use a private VIF to connect to the VPC in eu-west-1. Use two Direct Connect gateways, one for each VIF, to route from the Direct Connect locations to the corresponding AWS Region along the path that has the lowest latency.

C. Create one dedicated connection. Use a transit VIF to connect to the transit gateway in us-east-1. Use a private VIF to connect to the VPC in eu-west-1. Use one Direct Connect gateway for both VIFs to route from the Direct Connect locations to the corresponding AWS Region along the path that has the lowest latency.

D. Create one dedicated connection. Use a transit VIF to connect to the transit gateway in us-east-1. Use a private VIF to connect to the VPC in eu-west-1. Use two Direct Connect gateways, one for each VIF, to route from the Direct Connect locations to the corresponding AWS Region along the path that has the lowest latency.

16) A company recently moved its Amazon EC2 instances to VPC private subnets to comply with security requirements. The EC2 instances now rely on a NAT gateway for internet connectivity. Following the migration, certain lengthy database queries from private EC2 instances to a publicly accessible third-party database are not receiving responses. Analysis of the database query logs indicates that the queries were successfully processed after 7 minutes, but the client EC2 instances did not receive the responses.

Which configuration change should a network engineer implement to resolve this issue?

A. Configure the NAT gateway timeout to allow connections for up to 600 seconds.

B. Enable enhanced networking on the client EC2 instances.

C. Enable TCP keepalive on the client EC2 instances with a value of less than 300 seconds.

D. Close idle TCP connections through the NAT gateway.

17) A company launches a new web application on Amazon EC2 instances. The application is hosted in private subnets across three Availability Zones behind an Application Load Balancer (ALB). Security auditors mandate encryption for all connections. The company uses Amazon Route 53 for DNS and AWS Certificate Manager (ACM) for automated SSL/TLS certificate provisioning. SSL/TLS connections are terminated at the ALB.

During testing with a single EC2 instance, the application shows no issues. However, after deploying to production, users report being able to log in but unable to use the application. Each new web request restarts the login process.

What should a network engineer do to resolve this issue?

A. Modify the ALB listener configuration. Edit the rule that forwards traffic to the target group. Change the rule to enable group-level stickiness. Set the duration to the maximum application session length.

B. Replace the ALB with a Network Load Balancer. Create a TLS listener. Create a new target group with the protocol type set to TLS Register the EC2 instances. Modify the target group configuration by enabling the stickiness attribute.

C. Modify the ALB target group configuration by enabling the stickiness attribute. Use an application-based cookie. Set the duration to the maximum application session length.

D. Remove the ALB. Create an Amazon Route 53 rule with a failover routing policy for the application name. Configure ACM to issue certificates for each EC2 instance.

18) A company operates various workloads on Amazon EC2 instances located in public subnets. During a recent security

incident, an attacker exploited a vulnerability in one of the EC2 instances' applications to gain unauthorized access. The company promptly addressed the vulnerability by fixing the application and deploying a replacement EC2 instance with the updated application.

Subsequently, the attacker used the compromised application to distribute malware across the internet. The company was alerted to the compromise through a notification from AWS. To prevent such incidents in the future, the company requires the capability to detect when an application deployed on an EC2 instance is distributing malware.

Which solution will meet this requirement with the LEAST operational effort?

A. Use Amazon GuardDuty to analyze traffic patterns by inspecting DNS requests and VPC flow logs.

B. Use Amazon GuardDuty to deploy AWS managed decoy systems that are equipped with the most recent malware signatures.

C. Set up a Gateway Load Balancer. Run an intrusion detection system (IDS) appliance from AWS Marketplace on Amazon EC2 for traffic inspection.

D. Configure Amazon Inspector to perform deep packet inspection of outgoing traffic.

19) A company operates two AWS accounts: one for Production and one for Connectivity. A network engineer is tasked with establishing a connection between the VPC in the Production account and a transit gateway in the Connectivity account. The auto-acceptance of shared attachments feature is not enabled on the transit gateway.

Which set of steps should the network engineer follow in each AWS account to meet these requirements?

A. 1. In the Production account: Create a resource share in AWS Resource Access Manager for the transit gateway. Provide the Connectivity account ID. Enable the feature to allow external accounts.

2. In the Connectivity account: Accept the resource.
3. In the Connectivity account: Create an attachment to the VPC subnets.

4. In the Production account: Accept the attachment. Associate a route table with the attachment.

B. 1. In the Production account: Create a resource share in AWS Resource Access Manager for the VPC subnets. Provide the Connectivity account ID. Enable the feature to allow external accounts.

2. In the Connectivity account: Accept the resource.
3. In the Production account: Create an attachment on the transit gateway to the VPC subnets.

4. In the Connectivity account: Accept the attachment. Associate a route table with the attachment.

C. 1. In the Connectivity account: Create a resource share in AWS Resource Access Manager for the VPC subnets. Provide the Production account ID. Enable the feature to allow external accounts.

2. In the Production account: Accept the resource.
3. In the Connectivity account: Create an attachment on the transit gateway to the VPC subnets.

4. In the Production account: Accept the attachment. Associate a route table with the attachment.

D. 1. In the Connectivity account: Create a resource share in

AWS Resource Access Manager for the transit gateway. Provide the Production account ID Enable the feature to allow external accounts.

2. In the Production account: Accept the resource.
3. In the Production account: Create an attachment to the VPC subnets.

4. In the Connectivity account: Accept the attachment. Associate a route table with the attachment.

20) A company is preparing to deploy a two-tier web application in a new VPC within a single AWS Region. The VPC has been set up with an internet gateway and four subnets: two public subnets with default routes to the internet gateway, and two private subnets sharing a route table without a default route.

The application will be hosted on Amazon EC2 instances behind an external Application Load Balancer (ALB). These EC2 instances should not be directly accessible from the internet. The application will utilize an Amazon S3 bucket in the same Region for data storage, involving S3 GET and PUT API operations from the EC2 instances. The goal is to design a VPC architecture that minimizes data transfer costs.

Which solution will meet these requirements?

A. Deploy the EC2 instances in the public subnets. Create an S3 interface endpoint in the VPC. Modify the application configuration to use the S3 endpoint-specific DNS hostname.

B. Deploy the EC2 instances in the private subnets. Create a NAT gateway in the VPC. Create default routes in the private subnets to the NAT gateway. Connect to Amazon S3 by using the NAT gateway.

C. Deploy the EC2 instances in the private subnets. Create an S3 gateway endpoint in the VPSpecify die route table of the private subnets during endpoint creation to create routes to Amazon S3.

D. Deploy the EC2 instances in the private subnets. Create an S3 interface endpoint in the VPC. Modify the application configuration to use the S3 endpoint-specific DNS hostname.

21) Your security team has deployed a host-based firewall on all Amazon Elastic Compute Cloud (EC2) instances to block all outgoing traffic. Access to the instance metadata service is restricted, and exceptions must be requested for each specific requirement before access is granted.

Which firewall rule should you request to be added to your instances to allow instance metadata access?

A. Inbound; Protocol tcp; Source [Instance's EIP]; Destination 169.254.169.254

B. Inbound; Protocol tcp; Destination 169.254.169.254; Destination port 80

C. Outbound; Protocol tcp; Destination 169.254.169.254; Destination port 80

D. Outbound; Protocol tcp; Destination 169 .254.169.254; Destination port 443

22) All IP addresses in a 10.0.0.0/16 VPC are in use by application servers across two Availability Zones. These servers need to send frequent UDP probes to a central authentication server on the Internet to confirm that it is running up-to-date packages. The network is set up so that the application servers use a single NAT gateway for internal access. Testing has shown that some of the servers are unable

to communicate with the authentication server.

What is the reason for this failure?

A. The NAT gateway does not support UDP traffic.

B. The authentication server is not accepting traffic.

C. The NAT gateway cannot allocate more ports.

D. The NAT gateway is launched in a private subnet.

23) An organization is transitioning from a tape backup system to a storage gateway but currently lacks connectivity to AWS. They require initial testing to be conducted.

What connection option should the organization use to get up and running at minimal cost?

A. Use an internet connection.

B. Set up an AWS VPN connection.

C. Provision an AWS Direct Connection private virtual interface.

D. Provision a Direct Connect public virtual interface.

24) An organization has deployed an IPv6-only web portal to cater to IPv6-native mobile clients. Front-end instances are launched in an Amazon VPC that is associated with a suitable IPv6 CIDR. The VPC's IPv4 CIDR is fully utilized. Each of the two Availability Zones has a single subnet with properly configured IPv6 CIDR associations. Auto Scaling is correctly set up, and Elastic Load Balancing is not utilized. Customers have reported that the service is unavailable during peak load times.

The network engineer attempts to launch an instance

manually and receives the following message:

"There are not enough free addresses in subnet 'subnet-12345677' to satisfy the requested number of instances."

What action will resolve the availability problem?

A. Add a secondary IPv4 CIDR to the Amazon VPC. Assign secondary IPv4 address space to each of the existing subnets.

B. Create a new subnet using a VPC secondary IPv4 CIDR, and associate an IPv6 CIDR. Include the new subnet in the Auto Scaling group.

C. Resize the IPv6 CIDR on each of the existing subnets. Modify the Auto Scaling group maximum number of instances.

D. Create a new subnet using a VPC secondary IPv6 CIDR, and associate an IPv6 CIDR. Include the new subnet in the Auto Scaling group.

25) An organization is utilizing a VPC endpoint for Amazon S3. Initially, the security group rules for a group of instances were configured to restrict access, allowing traffic only to the IP addresses of the Amazon S3 API endpoints in the region from the published JSON file. The application was functioning correctly, but it is now experiencing an increasing number of timeouts when attempting to connect with Amazon S3. The VPC does not have an internet gateway configured.

Which solution will fix the connectivity failures with the LEAST amount of effort?

A. Create a Lambda function to update the security group based on AmazonIPSpaceChanged notifications.

B. Update the VPC routing to direct Amazon S3 prefix-list traffic to the VPC endpoint using the route table APIs.

C. Update the application server's outbound security group to use the prefix-list for Amazon S3 in the same region.

D. Create an additional VPC endpoint for Amazon S3 in the same route table to scale the concurrent connections to Amazon S3.

26) A bank has developed a new version of its banking application in AWS using containers that connect to an on-premises database via a VPN connection. This new application version requires users to update their client application. The bank intends to phase out the previous client version. However, the company aims to continue supporting older clients through their on-premises application version to accommodate a small portion of customers who have not yet upgraded.

What design will allow the company to serve both newer and earlier clients in the MOST efficient way?

A. Use an Amazon Route 53 multivalue answer routing policy to route older client traffic to the on-premises application version and the rest of the traffic to the new AWS based version.

B. Use a Classic Load Balancer for the new application. Route all traffic to the new application by using an Elastic Load Balancing (ELB) load balancer DNS. Define a user-agent-based rule on the backend servers to redirect earlier clients to the on-premises application.

C. Use an Application Load Balancer for the new application. Register both the new and earlier applications as separate target groups and use path-based routing to route traffic based on the application version.

D. Use an Application Load Balancer for the new application. Register both the new and earlier application backends as separate target groups. Use header-based routing to route traffic based on the application version.

27) A company is installing third-party firewall appliances in its VPC for traffic inspection and NAT capabilities. The VPC is set up with private and public subnets. The company intends to deploy the firewall appliances behind a load balancer.

Which architecture will meet these requirements MOST cost-effectively?

A. Utilize a Gateway Load Balancer with the firewall appliances as targets. Configure the firewall appliances with a single network interface in a private subnet. Employ a NAT gateway to direct the traffic to the internet post-inspection.

B. Deploy a Gateway Load Balancer with the firewall appliances as targets. Configure the firewall appliances with two network interfaces: one network interface in a private subnet and another network interface in a public subnet. Use the NAT functionality on the firewall appliances to send the traffic to the internet after inspection.

C. Deploy a Network Load Balancer with the firewall appliances as targets. Configure the firewall appliances with a single network interface in a private subnet. Use a NAT gateway to direct the traffic to the internet post-inspection.

D. Deploy a Network Load Balancer with the firewall appliances as targets. Configure the firewall appliances with two network interfaces: one in a private subnet and another in a public subnet. Utilize the NAT functionality on the firewall appliances to direct the traffic to the internet post-inspection.

28) A company's AWS architecture comprises multiple VPCs, including a shared services VPC and several application VPCs. Network connectivity has been established from all VPCs to the on-premises DNS servers.

Applications deployed in the application VPCs must be able to resolve DNS for internally hosted domains on premises. Additionally, these applications must be able to resolve local VPC domain names and domains hosted in Amazon Route 53 private hosted zones.

What should a network engineer do to meet these requirements?

A. Create a new Route 53 Resolver inbound endpoint in the shared services VPC. Create forwarding rules for the on-premises hosted domains. Associate the rules with the new Resolver endpoint and each application VPC. Update each application VPC's DHCP configuration to point DNS resolution to the new Resolver endpoint.

B. Create a new Route 53 Resolver outbound endpoint in the shared services VPC. Create forwarding rules for the on-premises hosted domains. Associate the rules with the new Resolver endpoint and each application VPC.

C. Create a new Route 53 Resolver outbound endpoint in the shared services VPCreate forwarding rules for the on-premises hosted domains. Associate the rules with the new Resolver endpoint and each application VPUpdate each application VPC's DHCP configuration to point DNS resolution to the new Resolver endpoint.

D. Create a new Route 53 Resolver inbound endpoint in the shared services VPC. Create forwarding rules for the on-premises hosted domains. Associate the rules with the new

Resolver endpoint and each application VPC.

29) A company has workloads running in a VPC that access Amazon S3 through an S3 gateway endpoint. Additionally, the company has on-premises workloads that require private access to Amazon S3 over a VPN connection, which has been established to the VPC.

Which solution will provide connectivity to Amazon S3 from the VPC workloads and the on-premises workloads in the MOST operationally efficient way?

A. Deploy a proxy fleet of Amazon EC2 instances in the VPC behind an Application Load Balancer (ALB). Configure the on-premises workloads to use the ALB as the proxy server to connect to Amazon S3. Configure the proxy fleet to use the S3 gateway endpoint to connect to Amazon S3.

B. Delete the S3 gateway endpoint. Create an S3 interface endpoint. Deploy a proxy fleet of Amazon EC2 instances in the VPC behind an Application Load Balancer (ALB).
Configure the on-premises workloads to use the ALB as the proxy server to connect to Amazon S3. Configure the proxy fleet and the VPC workloads to use the S3 interface
endpoint to connect to Amazon S3.

C. Create an S3 interface endpoint. Configure an on-premises DNS resolver to resolve the S3 DNS names to the private IP addresses of the S3 interface endpoint. Use the S3
interface endpoint to access Amazon S3. Continue to use the S3 gateway endpoint for the VPC workloads to access Amazon S3.

D. Set up an AWS Direct Connect connection. Create a public VIF. Configure on-premises routing to route the S3 traffic over the public VIF. Make no changes to the on-premises
workloads. Continue to use the S3 gateway endpoint for the VPC

workloads to access Amazon S3.

30) A company's VPC includes Amazon EC2 instances communicating with AWS services over the public internet, which they want to change. They deploy AWS PrivateLink endpoints in the VPC to facilitate this change. However, after deploying the PrivateLink endpoints, the EC2 instances can no longer communicate with the required AWS services at all.

Which combination of steps should a network engineer take to restore communication with the AWS services? (Select TWO.)

A. In the VPC route table, add a route that has the PrivateLink endpoints as the destination.

B. Ensure that the enableDnsSupport attribute is set to True for the VPC. Ensure that each VPC endpoint has DNS support enabled.

C. Ensure that the VPC endpoint policy allows communication.

D. Create an Amazon Route 53 public hosted zone for all services.

E. Create an Amazon Route 53 private hosted zone that includes a custom name for each service.

31) An insurance company is preparing to migrate workloads from its on-premises data center to the AWS Cloud. The company needs end-to-end domain name resolution and bi-directional DNS resolution between AWS and the existing on-premises environments. The workloads will be migrated to multiple VPCs, and they have dependencies on each other. The migration will not occur simultaneously for all workloads.

Which solution meets these requirements?

A. Configure a private hosted zone for each application VPC, and create the requisite records. Create a set of Amazon Route 53 Resolver inbound and outbound endpoints in an egress VPC. Define Route 53 Resolver rules to forward requests for the on-premises domains to the on-premises DNS resolver. Associate the application VPC private hosted zones with the egress VPC, and share the Route 53 Resolver rules with the application accounts by using AWS Resource Access Manager. Configure the on-premises DNS servers to forward the cloud domains to the Route 53 inbound endpoints.

B. Set up a public hosted zone for each application VPC and configure the necessary records. Create Amazon Route 53 Resolver inbound and outbound endpoints in an egress VPC. Define Route 53 Resolver rules to forward requests for the on-premises domains to the on-premises DNS resolver. Associate the private hosted zones of the application VPCs with the egress VPC and share the Route 53 Resolver rules with the application accounts using AWS Resource Access Manager. Configure the on-premises DNS servers to forward the cloud domains to the Route 53 inbound endpoints.

C. Establish a private hosted zone for each application VPC and configure the required records. Create Amazon Route 53 Resolver inbound and outbound endpoints in an egress VPC. Define Route 53 Resolver rules to forward requests for the on-premises domains to the on-premises DNS resolver. Associate the private hosted zones of the application VPCs with the egress VPC and share the Route 53 Resolver rules with the application accounts using AWS Resource Access Manager. Configure the on-premises DNS servers to forward the cloud domains to the Route 53 outbound endpoints.

D. Configure a private hosted zone for each application VPC and set up the necessary records. Create Amazon Route 53 Resolver inbound and outbound endpoints in an egress VPC. Define

Route 53 Resolver rules to forward requests for the on-premises domains to the on-premises DNS resolver. Associate the Route 53 outbound rules with the application VPCs and share the private hosted zones with the application accounts using AWS Resource Access Manager. Configure the on-premises DNS servers to forward the cloud domains to the Route 53 inbound endpoints.

32) A company's network engineer designs and tests VPC networks in a development account. The company requires monitoring of network resource changes, strict compliance with network security policies, and access to historical configurations of network resources.

Which solution will meet these requirements?

A. Create an Amazon EventBridge (Amazon CloudWatch Events) rule with a custom pattern to monitor the account for changes. Configure the rule to invoke an AWS Lambda function to identify noncompliant resources. Update an Amazon DynamoDB table with the changes that are identified.

B. Create custom metrics from Amazon CloudWatch logs. Use the metrics to invoke an AWS Lambda function to identify noncompliant resources. Update an Amazon DynamoDB table with the changes that are identified.

C. Record the current state of network resources by using AWS Config. Create rules that reflect the desired configuration settings. Set remediation for noncompliant resources.

D. Record the current state of network resources by using AWS Systems Manager Inventory. Use Systems Manager State Manager to enforce the desired configuration settings and to carry out remediation for noncompliant resources.

33) You deploy an Amazon EC2 instance running a web server into a subnet within a VPC. An Internet gateway is attached, and the main route table includes a default route (0.0.0.0/0) targeting the Internet gateway. The instance's security group is configured to allow:

Protocol: TCP

Port: 80 inbound, nothing outbound

The Network ACL for the subnet is configured to allow:

Protocol: TCP

Port: 80 inbound, nothing outbound

However, when you attempt to access the web server, there is no response.

Which additional step should you take to receive a successful response?

A. Add an entry to the security group outbound rules for Protocol: TCP, Port Range: 80

B. Add an entry to the security group outbound rules for Protocol: TCP, Port Range: 1024-65535

C. Add an entry to the Network ACL outbound rules for Protocol: TCP, Port Range: 80

D. Add an entry to the Network ACL outbound rules for Protocol: TCP, Port Range: 1024-65535

34) A network engineer is assessing the network setup for a global retail company. The company has an AWS Direct Connect connection between its on-premises data center and

the AWS Cloud. In the eu-west-2 Region, the company has multiple VPCs attached to a transit gateway.

Recently, the company provisioned several AWS resources in the eu-central-1 Region, within a single VPC located near its users in that area. The network engineer needs to connect the resources in eu-central-1 to both the on-premises data center and the resources in eu-west-2, while minimizing changes to the Direct Connect connection.

What should the network engineer do to meet these requirements?

A. Create a new virtual private gateway. Attach the new virtual private gateway to the VPC in eu-central-1. Use a transit VIF to connect the VPC and the Direct Connect router.

B. Create a new transit gateway in eu-central-1. Create a peering attachment request to the transit gateway in eu-west-2. Add a static route in the transit gateway route table in eu-central-1 to point to the transit gateway peering attachment. Accept the peering request. Add a static route in the transit gateway route table in eu-west-2 to point to the new transit gateway peering attachment.

C. Create a new transit gateway in eu-central-1. Use an AWS Site-to-Site VPN connection to peer both transit gateways. Add a static route in the transit gateway route table in eu-central-1 to point to the transit gateway VPN attachment. Add a static route in the transit gateway route table in eu-west-2 to point to the new transit gateway peering attachment.

D. Create a new virtual private gateway. Attach the new virtual private gateway to the VPC in eu-central-1. Use a public VIF to connect the VPC and the Direct Connect router.

35) A company has established connectivity between its on-

premises data center in Paris, France, and the AWS Cloud using an AWS Direct Connect connection. The company utilizes a transit VIF to connect the Direct Connect connection with a transit gateway hosted in the Europe (Paris) Region. The company hosts workloads in private subnets across several VPCs attached to the transit gateway.

Recently, the company acquired another corporation with on-premises workloads in an office building in Tokyo, Japan. The company needs to migrate these workloads to AWS while ensuring they have access to the existing workloads in Paris. Additionally, the company must establish connectivity between the Tokyo office building and the Paris data center.

In the Asia Pacific (Tokyo) Region, the company creates a new VPC with private subnets for migrating the workloads. The migration must be completed within 5 days, and the workloads cannot be directly accessible from the internet.

Which set of steps should a network engineer take to meet these requirements?

A. 1. Create public subnets in the Tokyo VPC to migrate the workloads into.

2. Configure an internet gateway for the Tokyo office to reach the Tokyo VPC.

3. Configure security groups on the Tokyo workloads to only allow traffic from the Tokyo office and the Paris workloads.

4. Create peering connections between the Tokyo VPC and the Paris VPCs.

5. Configure a VPN connection between the Paris data center and the Tokyo office by using existing routers.

B. 1. Configure a transit gateway in the Asia Pacific (Tokyo) Region. Associate this transit gateway with the Tokyo VPC.

2. Create peering connections between the Tokyo transit gateway and the Paris transit gateway.

3. Set up a new Direct Connect connection from the Tokyo office to the Tokyo transit gateway.

4. Configure routing on both transit gateways to allow data to flow between sites and the VPCs.

C. 1. Configure a transit gateway in the Asia Pacific (Tokyo) Region. Associate this transit gateway with the Tokyo VPC.

2. Create peering connections between the Tokyo transit gateway and the Paris transit gateway.

3. Configure an AWS Site-to-Site VPN connection from the Tokyo office. Set the Tokyo transit gateway as the target.

4. Configure routing on both transit gateways to allow data to flow between sites and the VPCs.

D. 1. Configure an AWS Site-to-Site VPN connection from the Tokyo office to the Paris transit gateway.

2. Create an association between the Paris transit gateway and the Tokyo VPC.

3. Configure routing on the Paris transit gateway to allow data to flow between sites and the VPCs.

36) A company has deployed a critical application on a fleet of Amazon EC2 instances behind an Application Load Balancer. This application must always be accessible on port 443 from the public internet. Recently, an outage occurred due to an incorrect change to the EC2 security group.

A network engineer needs to automate the verification of network connectivity between the public internet and the EC2 instances whenever there is a change to the security group. Additionally, the solution must notify the network engineer if

the change affects the connection.

Which solution will meet these requirements?

A. Enable VPC Flow Logs on the elastic network interface of each EC2 instance to capture REJECT traffic on port 443. Publish the flow log records to a log group in Amazon CloudWatch Logs. Create a CloudWatch Logs metric filter for the log group to monitor rejected traffic. Set up an alarm to notify the network engineer.

B. Enable VPC Flow Logs on the elastic network interface of each EC2 instance to capture all traffic on port 443. Publish the flow log records to a log group in Amazon CloudWatch Logs. Create a CloudWatch Logs metric filter for the log group to monitor all traffic. Set up an alarm to notify the network engineer.

C. Create a VPC Reachability Analyzer path for port 443, specifying the security group as the source and the EC2 instances as the destination. Create an Amazon Simple Notification Service (Amazon SNS) topic to notify the network engineer if a security group change affects the connection. Develop an AWS Lambda function to start Reachability Analyzer and publish a message to the SNS topic if the analysis fails. Create an Amazon EventBridge (Amazon CloudWatch Events) rule to trigger the Lambda function when a security group change occurs.

D. Create a VPC Reachability Analyzer path on port 443. Specify the internet gateway of the VPC as the source. Specify the EC2 instances as the destination. Create an Amazon Simple Notification Service (Amazon SNS) topic to notify the network engineer when a change to the security group affects the connection. Create an AWS Lambda function to start Reachability Analyzer and to publish a message to the SNS topic in case the analyses fail. Create an Amazon EventBridge (Amazon CloudWatch Events) rule to invoke the Lambda function when a change to the security group occurs.

37) A company operates two business units (BUs) in the us-east-1 and us-west-1 Regions, with plans to expand to additional Regions in the future. Each BU has a VPC in both Regions, and each Region has a transit gateway to which the BU VPCs are attached. The transit gateways in both Regions are peered.

As the company anticipates creating more BUs and needs to isolate certain BUs from others, it seeks to migrate to an architecture that can accommodate the expansion to more Regions and BUs.

Which solution will meet these requirements with the MOST operational efficiency?

A. Create a new transit gateway for each new BU in each Region. Peer the new transit gateways with the existing transit gateways. Update the route tables to control traffic between BUs.

B. Create an AWS Cloud WAN core network with an edge location in both Regions. Configure a segment for each BU with VPC attachments to the new BU VPCs. Use segment actions to control traffic between segments.

C. Create an AWS Cloud WAN core network with an edge location in both Regions. Configure a segment for each BU with VPC attachments to the new BU VPCs. Configure the segments to isolate attachments to control traffic between segments.

D. Attach new VPCs to the existing transit gateways. Update route tables to control traffic between BUs.

38) An AWS CloudFormation template is being utilized to establish a VPC peering connection between two operational

VPCs, each owned by a distinct AWS account. All required components in the 'Remote' (receiving) account have been configured and are ready. The template provided below facilitates the creation of the VPC peering connection in the Originating account.

It contains these components:

AWSTemplateFormation Version: 2010-09-09

Parameters:

Originating VCId:

Type: String

RemoteVPCId:

Type: String

RemoteVPCAccountld:

Type: String

Resources:

newVPCPeeringConnection:

Type: 'AWS::EC2::VPCPeeringConnection' Properties:

Vpcdld: !Ref OriginatingVPCId

PeerVpcld: !Ref Remote VPCId

PeerOwnerld: !Ref RemoteVPCAccountld

Which additional AWS CloudFormation components are required in the Originating account to establish an operational cross-account VPC peering connection with AWS CloudFormation? (Select two.)

A. Resources:

NewEC2 Security Group:

Type: AWS::EC2::SecurityGroup

B. Resources:

NetworkInterface To RemoteVPC:

Type: "AWS:: EC2NetworkInterface"

C. Resources:

newEC2Route:

Type: AWS::EC2::Route

D. Resources:

VPCGateway To Remote VPC:

Type: "AWS::EC2::VPCGatewayAttachment"

E. Resources:

newVPCPeeringConnection:

Type: 'AWS::EC2VPCPeeringConnection'

PeerRoleArn: !Ref PeerRoleArn

39) A company has a total of 30 VPCs, with 10 VPCs in each of three AWS Regions. The company has connected the VPCs in each Region to a transit gateway in that Region and has established inter-Region peering connections between the transit gateways.

The company intends to use AWS Direct Connect to grant access from its on-premises location to only four of the VPCs across the three Regions. The company has provisioned four Direct Connect connections at two Direct Connect locations.

Which combination of steps will meet these requirements MOST cost-effectively? (Choose three.)

A. Create four virtual private gateways. Attach the virtual private gateways to the four VPCs.

B. Create a Direct Connect gateway. Associate the four virtual private gateways with the Direct Connect gateway.

C. Create four transit VIFs on each Direct Connect connection. Associate the transit VIFs with the Direct Connect gateway.

D. Create four transit VIFs on each Direct Connect connection. Associate the transit VIFs with the four virtual private gateways.

E. Create four private VIFs on each Direct Connect connection to the Direct Connect gateway.

F. Create an association between the Direct Connect gateway and the transit gateways.

40) A development team is constructing a new web application in the AWS Cloud. The primary company domain, example.com, is presently housed in an Amazon Route 53 public hosted zone within one of the company's production AWS accounts.

The developers aim to trial the web application in the company's staging AWS account, utilizing publicly resolvable subdomains under the example.com domain. They require the capability to create and remove DNS records as necessary. Although developers have complete access to Route 53 hosted zones within the staging account, they are restricted from accessing resources in any of the production AWS accounts.

Which combination of steps should a network engineer take to allow the developers to create records under the example com domain? (Choose two.)

A. Create a public hosted zone for example com in the staging account

B. Create a staging example.com NS record in the example.com domain. Populate the value with the name servers from the staging.example.com domain. Set the routing policy type to simple routing.

C. Create a private hosted zone for staging example com in the staging account.

D. Create an example com NS record in the staging example.com domain. Populate the value with the name servers from the example.com domain. Set the routing policy type to simple routing.

E. Create a public hosted zone for staging.example.com in the staging account.

41) A company is creating an application where IoT devices will send measurements to the AWS Cloud. The application is expected to have millions of end users. The company has found that the IoT devices cannot handle DNS resolution. The company requires an Amazon EC2 Auto Scaling solution to allow the IoT devices to connect to an application endpoint without relying on DNS.

Which solution will meet these requirements MOST cost-effectively?

A. Use an Application Load Balancer (ALB)-type target group for a Network Load Balancer (NLB). Create an EC2 Auto Scaling group. Attach the Auto Scaling group to the ALB. Set up the IoT devices to connect to the IP addresses of the NLB.

B. Use an AWS Global Accelerator accelerator with an Application Load Balancer (ALB) endpoint. Create an EC2 Auto Scaling group. Attach the Auto Scaling group to the ALSet up the

IoT devices to connect to the IP addresses of the accelerator.

C. Use a Network Load Balancer (NLB). Create an EC2 Auto Scaling group. Attach the Auto Scaling group to the NLB. Set up the IoT devices to connect to the IP addresses of the NLB.

D. Use an AWS Global Accelerator accelerator with a Network Load Balancer (NLB) endpoint. Create an EC2 Auto Scaling group. Attach the Auto Scaling group to the NLB. Set up the IoT devices to connect to the IP addresses of the accelerator.

42) A company has launched a new web application on Amazon EC2 instances behind an Application Load Balancer (ALB). The instances are managed by an Amazon EC2 Auto Scaling group. The application will be used by enterprise customers globally. Employees of these enterprises will access the application over HTTPS from their office locations.

The company needs to set up firewalls to restrict outbound traffic to approved IP addresses only. The employees of the enterprise customers should be able to access the application with minimal latency.

Which change should a network engineer make in the infrastructure to meet these requirements?

A. Create a new Network Load Balancer (NLB). Add the ALB as a target of the NLB.

B. Create a new Amazon CloudFront distribution. Set the ALB as the distribution's origin.

C. Create a new accelerator in AWS Global Accelerator. Add the ALB as an accelerator endpoint.

D. Create a new Amazon Route 53 hosted zone. Create a new record to route traffic to the ALB.

43) The company operates hundreds of VPCs on AWS, all of which utilize NAT gateways to access the public endpoints of Amazon S3 and AWS Systems Manager. Traffic from the VPCs to these services is routed through the NAT gateways. The network engineer needs to consolidate access to these services and remove the necessity of utilizing public endpoints.

Which solution will meet these requirements with the LEAST operational overhead?

A. Create a central egress VPC that has private NAT gateways. Connect all the VPCs to the central egress VPC by using AWS Transit Gateway. Use the private NAT gateways to connect to Amazon S3 and Systems Manager by using private IP addresses.

B. Create a central shared services VPC. In the central shared services VPC, create interface VPC endpoints for Amazon S3 and Systems Manager to access. Ensure that private DNS is turned off. Connect all the VPCs to the central shared services VPC by using AWS Transit Gateway. Create an Amazon Route 53 forwarding rule for each interface VPC endpoint. Associate the forwarding rules with all the VPCs. Forward DNS queries to the interface VPC endpoints in the shared services VPC.

C. Create a central shared services VPIn the central shared services VPC, create interface VPC endpoints for Amazon S3 and Systems Manager to access. Ensure that private DNS is turned off. Connect all the VPCs to the central shared services VPC by using AWS Transit Gateway. Create an Amazon Route 53 private hosted zone with a full-service endpoint name for Amazon S3 and Systems Manager. Associate the private hosted zones with all the VPCs. Create an alias record in each private hosted zone with the full AWS service endpoint pointing to the interface VPC endpoint in the shared services VPC.

D. Create a central shared services VPC. In the central shared services VPC, create interface VPC endpoints for Amazon S3 and Systems Manager to access. Connect all the VPCs to the central shared services VPC by using AWS Transit Gateway. Ensure that private DNS is turned on for the interface VPC endpoints and that the transit gateway is created with DNS support turned on.

44) The company, which manages resources across multiple AWS Regions in various VPCs, requires the ability to connect to these resources using its internal domain name, aws.example.com.

What must the network engineer do to meet this requirement?

A. Create an Amazon Route 53 private hosted zone for aws.example.com in each Region that has resources. Associate the private hosted zone with that Region's VPC. In the appropriate private hosted zone, create DNS records for the resources in each Region.

B. Create one Amazon Route 53 private hosted zone for aws.example.com. Configure the private hosted zone to allow zone transfers with every VPC.

C. Create one Amazon Route 53 private hosted zone for example.com. Create a single resource record for aws.example.com in the private hosted zone. Apply a multivalue answer routing policy to the record. Add all VPC resources as separate values in the routing policy.

D. Create one Amazon Route 53 private hosted zone for aws.example.com. Associate the private hosted zone with every VPC that has resources. In the private hosted zone, create DNS records for all resources.

45) A global company operates business applications in the us-east-1 Region within a VPC. One of the company's

regional offices in London employs a virtual private gateway for an AWS Site-to-Site VPN connection to the VPC. The company has established a transit gateway and has arranged peering between the VPC and other VPCs used by different departments within the company.

Employees at the London office are encountering latency problems when accessing the business applications.

What should a network engineer do to reduce this latency?

A. Create a new Site-to-Site VPN connection. Set the transit gateway as the target gateway. Enable acceleration on the new Site-to-Site VPN connection. Update the VPN device in the London office with the new connection details.

B. Modify the existing Site-to-Site VPN connection by setting the transit gateway as the target gateway. Enable acceleration on the existing Site-to-Site VPN connection.

C. Create a new transit gateway in the eu-west-2 (London) Region. Peer the new transit gateway with the existing transit gateway. Modify the existing Site-to-Site VPN connection by setting the new transit gateway as the target gateway.

D. Create a new AWS Global Accelerator standard accelerator that has an endpoint of the Site-to-Site VPN connection. Update the VPN device in the London office with the new connection details.

46) The company operates a hybrid cloud environment, connecting its data center to the AWS Cloud via an AWS Direct Connect connection. Within AWS, the company uses a hub-and-spoke model to connect VPCs using a transit gateway. A transit VIF with a Direct Connect gateway provides connectivity to on-premises resources.

The company utilizes a hybrid DNS model, with Amazon Route 53 Resolver endpoints configured in the hub VPC for bidirectional DNS traffic. One of the VPCs hosts a backend application, and the company employs Amazon SQS in a message-oriented architecture to receive messages from other applications over a private network. The network engineer intends to use an interface VPC endpoint for Amazon SQS to facilitate this architecture, ensuring that client services can access the endpoint service from on premises and from multiple VPCs within the company's AWS infrastructure.

Which combination of steps should the network engineer take to ensure that the client applications can resolve DNS for the interface endpoint? (Choose three.)

A. Create the interface endpoint for Amazon SQS with the option for private DNS names turned on.

B. Create the interface endpoint for Amazon SQS with the option for private DNS names turned off.

C. Manually create a private hosted zone for sqs.us-east-1.amazonaws.com. Add necessary records that point to the interface endpoint. Associate the private hosted zones with other VPCs.

D. Use the automatically created private hosted zone for sqs.us-east-1.amazonaws.com with previously created necessary records that point to the interface endpoint. Associate the private hosted zones with other VPCs.

E. Access the SQS endpoint by using the public DNS name sqs.us-east-1 amazonaws.com in VPCs and on premises.

F. Access the SQS endpoint by using the private DNS name of the interface endpoint .sqs.us-east-1.vpce.amazonaws.com in VPCs and on premises.

47) The company is migrating an application from on-premises to AWS and will host it on Amazon EC2 instances in a single VPC. Throughout the migration, DNS queries from the EC2 instances must be able to resolve names of on-premises servers. This requirement is temporary and will no longer be needed after the 3-month migration period.

What should a network engineer do to meet these requirements with the LEAST amount of configuration?

A. Set up an AWS Site-to-Site VPN connection between on premises and AWS. Deploy an Amazon Route 53 Resolver outbound endpoint in the Region that is hosting the VPC.

B. Set up an AWS Direct Connect connection with a private VIF. Deploy an Amazon Route 53 Resolver inbound endpoint and a Route 53 Resolver outbound endpoint in the Region that is hosting the VPC.

C. Set up an AWS Client VPN connection between on premises and AWS. Deploy an Amazon Route 53 Resolver inbound endpoint in the VPC.

D. Set up an AWS Direct Connect connection with a public VIF. Deploy an Amazon Route 53 Resolver inbound endpoint in the Region that is hosting the VPC. Use the IP address that is assigned to the endpoint for connectivity to the on-premises DNS servers.

48) A company hosts an application on Amazon EC2 instances behind an Application Load Balancer, with the instances in an Amazon EC2 Auto Scaling group. Due to a recent change to a security group, external users are unable to access the application.

To prevent this downtime from occurring again, a network

engineer must implement a solution that automatically corrects noncompliant changes to security groups.

Which solution will meet these requirements?

A. Set up Amazon GuardDuty to identify differences between the intended and current security group configurations. Develop an AWS Systems Manager Automation runbook to correct noncompliant security groups.

B. Establish an AWS Config rule to identify differences between the intended and current security group configurations. Configure AWS OpsWorks for Chef to correct noncompliant security groups.

C. Configure Amazon GuardDuty to identify differences between the intended and current security group configurations. Use AWS OpsWorks for Chef to correct noncompliant security groups.

D. Configure an AWS Config rule to detect inconsistencies between the desired security group configuration and the current security group configuration. Create an AWS Systems Manager Automation runbook to remediate noncompliant security groups.

49) A company has been using an outdated application layer protocol for communication among applications. The company has decided to discontinue the use of this protocol and must migrate all applications to support a new protocol. Although both protocols are TCP-based, they use different port numbers.

After several months of effort, the company has migrated dozens of applications running on Amazon EC2 instances and in containers. The company believes that all applications

have been successfully migrated but wants to confirm this. A network engineer is tasked with verifying that no application is still using the old protocol.

Which solution will meet these requirements without causing any downtime?

A. Utilize Amazon Inspector along with its Network Reachability rules package. Wait for the analysis to complete to identify which EC2 instances are still actively listening on the old port.

B. Activate Amazon GuardDuty. Utilize the graphical visualizations to filter for traffic utilizing the port associated with the old protocol. Exclude all internet traffic to filter out instances where the same port is used as an ephemeral port.

C. Configure VPC flow logs to be delivered into an Amazon S3 bucket. Use Amazon Athena to query the data and to filter for the port number that is used by the old protocol.

D. Inspect all security groups that are assigned to the EC2 instances that host the applications. Remove the port of the old protocol if that port is in the list of allowed ports. Verify that the applications are operating properly after the port is removed from the security groups.

50) A company has established an AWS Site-to-Site VPN connection between its existing VPC and on-premises network. The VPC is associated with the default DHCP options set. Within the VPC, an application is running on an Amazon Linux 2 Amazon EC2 instance. This application needs to retrieve an Amazon RDS database secret stored in AWS Secrets Manager through a private VPC endpoint. Additionally, an on-premises application offers an internal RESTful API service accessible via the URL https://api.example.internal. Internal DNS resolution is provided by two on-premises Windows DNS

servers.

The application running on the EC2 instance needs to communicate with an internal API service deployed in the on-premises environment. However, when the application attempts to call the internal API service using its assigned hostname, the call fails. Conversely, when a network engineer tests the API service call from the same EC2 instance using the API service's IP address, the call succeeds.

What should the network engineer do to resolve this issue and prevent the same problem from affecting other resources in the VPC?

A. Create a new DHCP options set that specifies the on-premises Windows DNS servers. Associate the new DHCP options set with the existing VPC. Reboot the Amazon Linux 2 EC2 instance.

B. Create an Amazon Route 53 Resolver rule. Associate the rule with the VPC. Configure the rule to forward DNS queries to the on-premises Windows DNS servers if the domain name matches example.internal.

C. Update the hosts file on the Amazon Linux 2 EC2 instance in the VPC to map the service domain name (api.example.internal) to the IP address of the internal API service.

D. Update the /etc/resolv.conf file on the Amazon Linux 2 EC2 instance in the VPC. Replace the IP addresses of the existing name servers in the file with the IP addresses of the company's on-premises Windows DNS servers.

51) A company has multiple production applications distributed across various AWS accounts in the us-east-1 Region. Access to these applications is restricted to specific partner companies. The applications are hosted on Amazon EC2 instances within an Auto Scaling group behind an

Application Load Balancer (ALB). These EC2 instances reside in private subnets and accept traffic exclusively from the ALB. The ALB, located in a public subnet, permits inbound traffic solely from partner network IP address ranges on port 80.

When the company adds a new partner, they need to include the IP address range of the partner network in the security group associated with the ALB in each account. To simplify this process, a network engineer needs to implement a solution for centralized management of the partner network IP address ranges.

Which solution will meet these requirements in the MOST operationally efficient manner?

A. Set up an Amazon DynamoDB table to store all IP address ranges and corresponding security groups requiring updates. When a new partner is added, update the DynamoDB table with the new IP address range. Use an AWS Lambda function to periodically check the DynamoDB table for new IP address ranges and update the security groups accordingly. Implement this solution across all accounts.

B. Create a new prefix list containing all authorized IP address ranges. Utilize Amazon EventBridge (Amazon CloudWatch Events) rules to trigger an AWS Lambda function for updating security groups whenever a new IP address range is added to the prefix list. Deploy this solution across all accounts.

C. Create a new prefix list. Add all allowed IP address ranges to the prefix list. Share the prefix list across different accounts by using AWS Resource Access Manager (AWS RAM). Update security groups to use the prefix list instead of the partner IP address range. Update the prefix list with the new IP address range when the company adds a new partner.

D. Create an Amazon S3 bucket to maintain all IP address ranges and security groups that need to be updated. Update the S3 bucket with the new IP address range when the company adds a new partner. Invoke an AWS Lambda function to read new IP address ranges and security groups from the S3 bucket to update the security groups. Deploy this solution in all accounts.

52) A company utilizes a 1 Gbps AWS Direct Connect connection to link its AWS environment to its on-premises data center, providing employees with access to an application VPC hosted on AWS. Many remote employees utilize a company-provided VPN to connect to the data center. These employees have reported experiencing slowness when accessing the application during business hours. Similar slowness has been reported by on-premises users while they are in the office.

The company plans to develop an additional application on AWS, which will be used by both on-site and remote employees. Following the deployment of this additional application, the company anticipates needing 20% more bandwidth than it currently uses. With the increased usage, the company aims to enhance resiliency in its AWS connectivity. A network engineer must assess the current implementation and make improvements within a limited budget.

What should the network engineer do to meet these requirements MOST cost-effectively?

A. Set up a new 1 Gbps Direct Connect dedicated connection to accommodate the additional traffic load from remote employees and the additional application. Create a link aggregation group (LAG).

B. Deploy an AWS Site-to-Site VPN connection to the application VPC. Configure the on-premises routing for the remote employees to connect to the Site-to-Site VPN connection.

C. Deploy Amazon Workspaces into the application VPInstruct the remote employees to connect to Workspaces.

D. Replace the existing 1 Gbps Direct Connect connection with two new 2 Gbps Direct Connect hosted connections. Create an AWS Client VPN endpoint in the application VPC. Instruct the remote employees to connect to the Client VPN endpoint.

53) A company with a global network uses transit gateways to connect AWS Regions. The company is experiencing an issue where two Amazon EC2 instances in different Regions cannot communicate with each other. A network engineer is tasked with troubleshooting this connectivity issue.

What should the network engineer do to meet this requirement?

A. Utilize AWS Network Manager Route Analyzer to examine routes in the transit gateway route tables and VPC route tables. Analyze the IP traffic accepted or rejected by security group rules and network ACL rules in the VPC using VPC flow logs.

B. Utilize AWS Network Manager Route Analyzer to examine routes in the transit gateway route tables. Verify the correctness of VPC route tables. Analyze the IP traffic accepted or rejected by security group rules and network ACL rules in the VPC using AWS Firewall Manager.

C. Use AWS Network Manager Route Analyzer to analyze routes in the transit gateway route tables. Verify that the VPC route tables are correct. Use VPC flow logs to analyze the IP traffic that security group rules and network ACL rules accept or reject in the VPC.

D. Use VPC Reachability Analyzer to analyze routes in the transit gateway route tables. Verify that the VPC route tables are correct. Use VPC flow logs to analyze the IP traffic that security group rules and network ACL rules accept or reject in the VPC.

54) A company requires a dedicated bandwidth connection to transfer data between its VPC and on-premises data center. The data must be encrypted in transit. The company has been collaborating with an AWS Partner Network (APN) Partner to set up the connection.
Which combination of steps will meet these requirements? (Choose three.)

A. Request a hosted connection from the APN Partner.

B. Request a hosted public VIF from the APN Partner.

C. Create an AWS Site-to-Site VPN connection.

D. Create an AWS Client VPN connection.

E. Create a private VIF.

F. Create a public VIF.

55) A company's security policy requires all outbound traffic from a VPC to its on-premises data center to traverse a security appliance, which is hosted on an Amazon EC2 instance. A network engineer must enhance the network performance between the on-premises data center and the security appliance.

Which actions should the network engineer take to meet these requirements? (Choose two.)

A. Use an EC2 instance that supports enhanced networking.

B. Send outbound traffic through a transit gateway.

C. Increase the EC2 instance size.

D. Place the EC2 instance in a placement group within the VPC.

E. Attach multiple elastic network interfaces to the EC2 instance.

56) AnyCompany has acquired Example Corp. AnyCompany's infrastructure is entirely on-premises, while Example Corp's infrastructure is entirely in the AWS Cloud. The companies are using AWS Direct Connect with AWS Transit Gateway to establish connectivity between them.

Example Corp has deployed a new application across two Availability Zones in a VPC without an internet gateway. The VPC's CIDR range is 10.0.0.0/16. Example Corp needs to access an application deployed on-premises by AnyCompany. Due to compliance requirements, Example Corp must access the application through a limited, contiguous block of approved IP addresses (10.1.0.0/24).

A network engineer needs to implement a highly available solution to achieve this goal. The network engineer starts by updating the VPC to add a new CIDR range of 10.1.0.0/24.

What should the network engineer do next to meet the requirements?

A. Divide the allowed IP address range and create subnets in each Availability Zone (AZ) within the VPC. Establish a public NAT gateway in each new subnet. Modify the route tables associated with existing subnets to direct application traffic to the public NAT gateway in the respective AZ. Additionally, configure a route in the route table linked to the public NAT gateways' subnets to forward traffic intended for the application to the transit gateway.

B. In each Availability Zone in the VPC, create a subnet that uses part of the allowed IP address range. Create a private NAT gateway in each of the new subnets. Update the route tables that are associated with other subnets to route application traffic to the private NAT gateway in the corresponding Availability Zone. Add a route to the route table that is associated with the subnets of the private NAT gateways to send traffic destined for the application to the transit gateway.

C. Within the VPC, establish a subnet utilizing the approved IP address range. Deploy a private NAT gateway in this new subnet. Modify the route tables associated with other subnets to direct application traffic towards the private NAT gateway. Additionally, configure a route in the route table linked to the private NAT gateway's subnet to forward traffic intended for the application to the transit gateway.

D. Within the VPC, create a subnet that uses the approved IP address range. Configure a public NAT gateway within this new subnet. Update the route tables associated with other subnets to route application traffic to the public NAT gateway. Add a route to the route table associated with the public NAT gateway's subnet to direct traffic destined for the application to the transit gateway.

57) A company utilizing Amazon Route 53 for DNS services seeks to enhance its DNS infrastructure for improved security.

The security team has configured DNS Security Extensions (DNSSEC) for the domain and wants clarification from the network engineer regarding the party responsible for rotating DNSSEC keys.

Which explanation should the network administrator provide to the security team?

A. AWS rotates the zone-signing key (ZSK). The company rotates the key-signing key (KSK).

B. The company rotates the zone-signing key (ZSK) and the key-signing key (KSK).

C. AWS rotates the AWS Key Management Service (AWS KMS) key and the key-signing key (KSK).

D. The company rotates the AWS Key Management Service (AWS KMS) key. AWS rotates the key-signing key (KSK).

58) A company is preparing to move an internal application to the AWS Cloud, with the application running on Amazon EC2 instances within a single VPC. Users will access the application from the company's on-premises data center through either AWS VPN or AWS Direct Connect. The application's endpoint will use a private domain name reserved specifically for AWS Cloud use.

To ensure high availability, each EC2 instance must have automatic failover to another EC2 instance within the same AWS account and VPC. The network engineer needs to design a DNS solution that does not expose the application to the public internet.

Which solution will meet these requirements?

A. Assign public IP addresses to the EC2 instances. Create an Amazon Route 53 private hosted zone for the AWS reserved domain name. Associate the private hosted zone with the VPC. Configure conditional forwarding in the on-premises DNS resolvers to forward all DNS queries for the AWS domain to the Route 53 Resolver outbound endpoint. In the private hosted zone, set up primary and failover records pointing to the public IP addresses of the EC2 instances. Create an Amazon CloudWatch metric and alarm to monitor the application's health, and set up a health check on the alarm for the primary application endpoint.

B. Deploy the EC2 instances in private subnets. Create an

Amazon Route 53 public hosted zone for the AWS reserved domain name and associate it with the VPC. Configure conditional forwarding in the on-premises DNS resolvers to forward all DNS queries for the AWS domain to the Route 53 Resolver inbound endpoint. In the public hosted zone, configure primary and failover records pointing to the IP addresses of the EC2 instances. Create an Amazon CloudWatch metric and alarm to monitor the application's health, and set up a health check on the alarm for the primary application endpoint.

C. Place the EC2 instances in private subnets. Create an Amazon Route 53 private hosted zone for the AWS reserved domain name. Associate the private hosted zone with the VPCreate a Route 53 Resolver inbound endpoint. Configure conditional forwarding in the on-premises DNS resolvers to forward all DNS queries for the AWS domain to the inbound endpoint IP address for Route 53 Resolver. In the private hosted zone, configure primary and failover records that point to the IP addresses of the EC2 instances. Create an Amazon CloudWatch metric and alarm to monitor the application's health. Set up a health check on the alarm for the primary application endpoint.

D. Place the EC2 instances in private subnets. Create an Amazon Route 53 private hosted zone for the AWS reserved domain name. Associate the private hosted zone with the VPC. Create a Route 53 Resolver inbound endpoint. Configure conditional forwarding in the on-premises DNS resolvers to forward all DNS queries for the AWS domain to the inbound endpoint IP address for Route 53 Resolver. In the private hosted zone, configure primary and failover records that point to the IP addresses of the EC2 instances. Set up Route 53 health checks on the private IP addresses of the EC2 instances.

59) A company is using an Amazon CloudFront distribution with an Application Load Balancer (ALB) as the origin. The network engineer needs to ensure that all incoming traffic

to the ALB originates from CloudFront. The solution should be implemented at the network layer rather than within the application.

Which solution will meet these requirements in the MOST operationally efficient way?

A. Add an inbound rule to the ALB's security group to allow the AWS managed prefix list for CloudFront.

B. Add an inbound rule to the network ACLs that are associated with the ALB's subnets. Use the AWS managed prefix list for CloudFront as the source in the rule.

C. Configure CloudFront to add a custom HTTP header to the requests that CloudFront sends to the ALB.

D. Associate an AWS WAF web ACL with the ALB. Configure the AWS WAF rules to allow traffic from the CloudFront IP set. Automatically update the CloudFront IP set by using an AWS Lambda function.

60) A company has applications deployed in a single AWS Region and its on-premises data center in a hybrid configuration. The company maintains a 1 Gbps AWS Direct Connect connection between the data center and AWS, which is currently 65% utilized.

The company is an AWS Enterprise Support plan subscriber. They are preparing to deploy a new critical application on AWS that will integrate with existing applications running in the data center.

The application SLA requires a minimum of 99.9% network uptime between the data center and AWS.

What is the MOST cost-effective way to meet this SLA requirement?

A. Terminate the existing 1 Gbps Direct Connect connection.

B. Establish two new hosted Direct Connect connections, each with a capacity of 500 Mbps, through an AWS Direct Connect partner. Configure two virtual interfaces (VIFs) for the existing VPC on both Direct Connect connections and implement BGP for load balancing.

C. Add a second virtual interface (VIF) to the current Direct Connect connection and connect it to the existing VPC. Implement BGP for load balancing between the VIFs in active/active mode.

D. Acquire an additional 1 Gbps Direct Connect connection from AWS in a different cross-connect location terminated in the associated Region. Set up a new virtual interface (VIF) for the existing VPC and utilize BGP for load balancing.

E. Purchase an additional 1 Gbps Direct Connect connection from AWS in the existing cross-connect location. Ask AWS to terminate this new connection in a different router. Provision two virtual interfaces (VIFs) to the same VPC on both Direct Connect connections, and use BGP for load balancing.

61) AWS CloudTrail can be configured to ___ log files across multiple accounts and regions so that log files are delivered to a single bucket.

A. aggregate

B. replicate

C. encrypt

D. disperse

62) Which services are appropriate for storing session state data for a highly available web application using stateless web servers? (Select TWO.)

A. CloudWatch

B. Storage Gateway

C. Elastic Load Balancing

D. DynamoDB

E. ElastiCache

63) A company stores an access key (access key ID and secret access key) in a text file on a custom Amazon Machine Image (AMI). The access key is used to access DynamoDB tables from instances created from the AMI. The security team has mandated a more secure solution.

Which solution will meet the security team's mandate?

A. Pass the access key to the instances through instance user data.

B. Put the access key in an S3 bucket, and retrieve the access key on boot from the instance.

C. Create an IAM role with permissions to access the table, and launch all instances with the new role.

D. Obtain the access key from a key server launched in a private subnet.

64) An application needs a highly available relational database with an initial storage capacity of 8 TB. The database will

increase by 8 GB daily. To handle expected traffic, at least eight read replicas will be necessary for database reads.

Which option will meet these requirements?

A. Amazon Aurora

B. DynamoDB

C. Amazon S3

D. Amazon Redshift

65) A Solutions Architect is designing a critical business application with a relational database that runs on an EC2 instance. It requires a single EBS volume capable of supporting up to 16,000 IOPS.

Which Amazon EBS volume type can meet the performance requirements of this application?

A. EBS Throughput Optimized HDD

B. EBS Provisioned IOPS SSD

C. EBS Cold HDD

D. EBS General Purpose SSD

ANSWERS AND EXPLANATION

1) The best architectural change for the most scalable DNS service is:

C. Create Route 53 Resolver outbound endpoints. Create Route 53 Resolver rules to forward queries to on-premises DNS servers for on-premises hosted domain names. Reconfigure the HPC cluster nodes to use the default VPC resolver instead of the EC2 instance-based DNS servers. Terminate the EC2 instances.

Here's why this option is the most scalable:

Managed Service: Route 53 Resolver is a managed DNS resolution service that is highly scalable and fault-tolerant. It eliminates the need to manage and maintain EC2 instances for DNS resolution.

Offloading Work: By using Route 53 Resolver, the HPC cluster nodes offload DNS resolution to a dedicated service, improving their performance and freeing up resources.

On-premises Forwarding: Route 53 Resolver rules can be created to forward specific queries (e.g., on-premises domains) to the on-premises DNS servers, ensuring proper resolution for both internal and external resources.

Centralized Management: The default VPC resolver simplifies configuration and management compared to managing multiple EC2 instances as DNS servers.

Cost-effective: Terminating the EC2 instances frees up resources and potentially reduces costs associated with running additional instances.

Scaling up EC2 instances (Option B) doesn't address the core issue of scalability and might not handle peak loads effectively.

Scaling out additional EC2 instances (Option A) adds complexity and is not as reliable as a managed service.

Forwarding all queries to on-premises servers (Option D) create a single point of failure and introduces network latency for resolving AWS resources.

Therefore, Option C provides a highly scalable, managed, and cost-effective solution for the data analytics company's DNS needs.

2) The correct answer is:

B. Set the BGP community tag for all prefixes from the primary data center to 7224:7300. Set the BGP community tag for all prefixes from the failover data center to 7224:7100.

Explanation:

In AWS Direct Connect, BGP (Border Gateway Protocol) community tags can influence routing decisions. Lower community tag values indicate higher preference.

7224:7100 has a higher preference than 7224:7300.

By setting the BGP community tag for all prefixes from the primary data center to 7224:7300 and for the failover data center to 7224:7100, you ensure the following:

Primary Data Center (7224:7300): This tag has a lower preference compared to 7224:7100.

Failover Data Center (7224:7100): This tag has a higher

preference, meaning traffic will be routed here if the primary data center is not reachable.

Thus, this configuration ensures that traffic from AWS is first routed to the primary data center. Only if the primary data center is unavailable will the traffic be routed to the failover data center.

Set the BGP community tag for all prefixes from the primary data center to 7224:7300, and set the BGP community tag for all prefixes from the failover data center to 7224:7100. This way, the primary data center will have a lower BGP local preference, making it the preferred path. If there is an outage in the primary data center, the failover data center will have a higher BGP local preference and will become the preferred path. The other options do not provide the correct community tag values for the primary and failover data centers.

References:

https://repost.aws/knowledge-center/direct-connect-bgp-communities

Direct Connect supports local preference BGP community tags to control the route preference of traffic on private and transit virtual interfaces. Direct Connect supports the following local preference BGP communities: 7224:7100 Low preference, 7224:7200 Medium preference, and 7224:7300 High preference1. Direct Connect evaluates local preference BGP community tags from lowest to highest preference. For each prefix that you advertise over a BGP session, you can apply a community tag to indicate the associated path's priority for returning traffic1.

See section "Local preference BGP communities" from:

https://docs.aws.amazon.com/directconnect/latest/UserGuide/

routing-and-bgp.html

3) The most cost-effective solution for the real estate company to collect Workspaces DNS queries for SIEM analysis is:

D. Configure Amazon Route 53 query logging. Set the destination as an Amazon Kinesis Data Firehose delivery stream that is configured to push data to the SIEM system.

Here's why this option is the most cost-effective:

Granular Logging: Route 53 query logging specifically captures DNS queries, providing the necessary data for the SIEM system without unnecessary traffic information.

Centralized Collection: Route 53 query logging aggregates data from all seven VPCs into a single stream, simplifying analysis and reducing complexity.

Push Delivery: Kinesis Data Firehose pushes the logs directly to the SIEM system, minimizing the need for polling and reducing load on the S3 bucket (Option A).

Cost-Effectiveness: Compared to VPC Flow Logs (Option A) that capture all traffic and CloudWatch Logs with Kinesis (Option B) which might require additional processing, Route 53 query logging is specifically designed for DNS queries and avoids unnecessary data collection, potentially reducing storage and processing costs.

Scalability: Route 53 query logging scales automatically to accommodate the company's needs as the number of Workspaces grows.

While other options might achieve the functionality:

Option A: VPC Flow Logs capture all traffic, generating a large amount of data that needs processing and increasing storage costs. Polling S3 can add latency and complexity.

Option B: CloudWatch Logs require additional configuration for filtering and pushing data to Kinesis, adding complexity.

Option C: VPC Traffic Mirroring copies all network traffic for each Workspace, creating a significant amount of data transfer and potentially overwhelming the SIEM system.

Therefore, Route 53 query logging with Kinesis Data Firehose offers a targeted, centralized, and cost-effective approach for collecting and delivering Workspaces DNS queries to the SIEM system.

Reference:

https://docs.aws.amazon.com/Route53/latest/DeveloperGuide/resolver-query-logs-choosing-target-resource.html

4) The best design for achieving low-latency, private connectivity between the US and European data centers/Regions is:

B. Connect the VPC in eu-west-2 to a new transit gateway. Connect the Europe data center to the new transit gateway by using a Direct Connect gateway and a new transit VIF. Associate the transit gateway in us-east-1 with the same Direct Connect gateway. Enable SiteLink for both transit VIFs. Peer the two transit gateways.

Here's why this option offers the lowest latency and efficient connectivity:

Dedicated Transit Gateway in eu-west-2: A separate transit gateway in eu-west-2 keeps regional traffic localized, reducing latency compared to routing everything through the US transit gateway (Option A & D).

Single Direct Connect Gateway: Utilizing the existing Direct Connect gateway in the US avoids unnecessary complexity and simplifies management.

SiteLink on Transit VIFs: Enabling SiteLink optimizes traffic flow between the on-premises data centers and their respective transit gateways.

Transit Gateway Peering: Peering the two transit gateways establishes a private, high-bandwidth connection for inter-region communication between the US and European workloads, minimizing latency compared to internet-based connections.

The other options have drawbacks:

Option A: Sharing a single transit gateway between regions increases traffic flow and potential latency.

Option C: Creating a new Direct Connect gateway in the US adds unnecessary complexity and doesn't improve latency compared to using the existing one.

Option D: Sharing a single transit gateway and using a private VIF in eu-west-2 might not fully isolate regional traffic, potentially impacting latency.

Therefore, Option B provides the most efficient and low-latency design for the company's network architecture.

Reference:

Below link (Figure 9) explains:

https://aws.amazon.com/blogs/networking-and-content-delivery/introducing-aws-direct-connect-sitelink/

5) The most efficient and secure approach for centralized KMS access with VPC endpoints in a Transit Gateway environment is:

A. In the shared services account, create an interface endpoint for AWS KMS. Modify the interface endpoint by disabling the private DNS name. Create a private hosted zone in the shared services account with an alias record that points to the interface endpoint. Associate the private hosted zone with the spoke VPCs in each AWS account.

Here's why this option is the best solution:

Centralized Management: Creating the interface endpoint and private hosted zone in the shared services account centralizes management and simplifies administration for the network services team.

Private DNS disabled: Disabling private DNS on the interface endpoint prevents automatic DNS resolution within the shared services VPC, promoting security and proper routing.

Shared Hosted Zone: A single private hosted zone in the shared services account acts as a central point of reference for all spoke VPCs.

Alias Record: The alias record in the shared hosted zone points to the interface endpoint, enabling spoke VPCs to resolve KMS access through the private hosted zone instead of the public internet.

Association with Spoke VPCs: Associating the shared hosted zone with the spoke VPCs allows resources within those VPCs to utilize the alias record for private KMS access.

The other options have drawbacks:

Option B & C: Creating interface endpoints and private hosted zones in each spoke account introduces unnecessary complexity and management overhead.

Option D: A single shared hosted zone with alias records pointing to individual spoke VPC's interface endpoints creates a less efficient design. Spoke VPCs would need to know the specific alias record for their KMS endpoint.

Therefore, Option A provides a centralized, secure, and manageable solution for centralized KMS access with VPC endpoints in the company's Transit Gateway environment.

Option A creates a private hosted zone in the shared services account with an alias record that points to the interface endpoint, and associates the private hosted zone with the spoke VPCs in each AWS account. Disabling the private DNS name of the interface endpoint ensures that DNS resolution of the endpoint is restricted to the Amazon Route 53 private hosted zone. This option creates a centralized model for managing interface endpoints and Route 53 zones in a shared services AWS account, which simplifies administration and reduces complexity.

6) To achieve the desired isolation and communication requirements with the minimum number of transit gateway route tables, the network engineer should perform a combination of the following actions:

C. Configure a separate transit gateway route table for all application VPCs. Associate all application VPCs with this transit route table. Propagate the shared services VPC attachment and the VPN attachment to this transit gateway route table.

E. Configure a separate transit gateway route table for on-premises and the shared services VPC. Associate the VPN attachment and the shared services VPC attachment with this transit gateway route table. Propagate all application VPC attachments to this transit gateway route table.

Here's why this combination meets the requirements:

Application VPC Isolation: All application VPCs are associated with the same transit gateway route table, keeping them isolated from each other (requirement 1).

On-premises and Shared Services: The separate route table for on-premises and shared services allows them to communicate with all application VPCs while keeping the application VPCs isolated from each other (requirement 2 & 3).

Minimum Number of Route Tables: This configuration uses only two route tables, minimizing complexity.

Let's explore why other options are not ideal:

Option A: Propagating all application VPC attachments to the on-premises route table would allow application VPCs to see each other's traffic, violating the isolation requirement.

Option B: Creating a separate route table for each application VPC is unnecessary and creates excessive management overhead.

Option D: Isolates the shared services VPC from application VPCs, contradicting requirement 3.

Reference:

https://docs.aws.amazon.com/vpc/latest/tgw/transit-gateway-isolated-shared.html

7) The correct route table configuration on the transit gateway

to meet the requirements is:

A. Configure a route table with the production and nonproduction VPC attachments associated with propagated routes for only the shared services VPC. Create an additional route table with only the shared services VPC attachment associated with propagated routes from the production and nonproduction VPCs.

Explanation:

This configuration ensures that:

Production and Nonproduction VPCs can communicate with the Shared Services VPC.

There is no direct communication between the Production and Nonproduction VPCs.

Explanation for other options:

B. This option would allow communication between all VPCs, including Production and Nonproduction, which is not desired.

C. This option would allow communication between all VPCs, including Production and Nonproduction, which is not desired.

D. This option would not allow communication between the VPCs, including Production and Nonproduction, which is not desired.

8) The correct answer is:

B. Configure a transit gateway in the same AWS Region as the existing virtual private gateway. Create a new accelerated Site-to-Site VPN connection. Connect the new connection to the transit gateway by using a VPN attachment. Update the customer gateway device to use the new Site-to-Site VPN connection. Delete the existing Site-to-Site VPN connection.

Explanation:

This solution involves setting up a transit gateway in the same AWS Region as the existing virtual private gateway. By creating a new accelerated Site-to-Site VPN connection and connecting it to the transit gateway using a VPN attachment, traffic can be optimized and congestion issues reduced. Updating the customer gateway device to use the new VPN connection and deleting the existing one ensures a smooth transition with minimal administration effort.

Reference:

Acceleration is only supported for Site-to-Site VPN connections that are attached to a transit gateway. Virtual private gateways do not support accelerated VPN connections.

https://docs.aws.amazon.com/vpn/latest/s2svpn/accelerated-vpn.html

9) The best solution for high-bandwidth, low-latency connectivity with minimal overhead between the company's infrastructure in ap-southeast-2 and the new environment in us-west-1 is:

B. Peer the transit gateways in each Region. Configure routing between the two transit gateways for each Region's IP addresses.

Here's why this option offers the most efficient solution:

Transit Gateway Peering: Peering the existing transit gateways in both Regions establishes a private, high-bandwidth connection for inter-region communication.

BGP Routing: Transit Gateway peering leverages BGP routing by default, allowing for dynamic and efficient traffic routing between the two Regions.

Scalability: Transit Gateway peering scales automatically to accommodate traffic demands.

Reduced Overhead: Compared to managing VPN connections (Option A & C), peering simplifies management and reduces operational overhead.

Let's explore why other options are not ideal:

Option A: While VPN connections can work, they might not provide the same level of bandwidth and might require additional configuration and management overhead compared to peering.

Option C: Setting up VPN servers in each Region introduces additional infrastructure and complexity. Routing traffic through VPN servers might also introduce latency compared to peering.

Option D: Attaching VPCs in us-west-1 to the transit gateway in ap-southeast-2 would route all traffic through the ap-southeast-2 Region, creating significant latency for US-based users.

Therefore, peering the transit gateways provides a high-performance, scalable, and operationally efficient solution for inter-region connectivity in this scenario.

10) The best approach to ensure DNS query resolution even if Route 53 Resolver DNS Firewall becomes unresponsive is:

B. Update the DNS Firewall VPC configuration to enable fail open for the VPC.

Here's why this option meets the requirements:

Fail Open: Enabling fail open in the Route 53 Resolver DNS Firewall configuration instructs Resolver to allow DNS queries to proceed even if it doesn't receive a response from the firewall. This ensures that even during firewall outages, applications within the VPC can still resolve DNS queries.

Upholding SLAs: By allowing query resolution even in case of firewall issues, this approach helps maintain application availability and service level agreements (SLAs).

Let's see why other options are not ideal:

Option A: Disabling fail open would completely block DNS queries if the firewall is unresponsive, potentially causing application outages and violating SLAs.

Option C & D: DHCP options sets are not used to configure fail open behavior for Route 53 Resolver DNS Firewall. These options are typically used to configure DHCP servers and related settings.

Therefore, enabling fail open in the DNS Firewall VPC configuration provides the desired functionality for maintaining DNS resolution during potential firewall outages.

Enabling the "fail open" feature in the Route 53 Resolver DNS Firewall VPC configuration ensures that if DNS Firewall becomes unresponsive, DNS queries will still be resolved. This helps maintain application service level agreements by allowing resources in the VPC to continue operating even if Route 53 Resolver does not receive a response from DNS Firewall.

Reference:

https://docs.aws.amazon.com/Route53/latest/DeveloperGuide/resolver-dns-firewall-vpc-configuration.html

11) To achieve secure, reliable, and high-bandwidth connectivity for the financial company, the network team should implement a combination of the following:

B. Set up an AWS Direct Connect connection from one of the company's data centers to us-east-1 and us-west-2.

E. Set up a transit VIF for an AWS Direct Connect gateway to send data to Amazon S3. Create a transit gateway. Associate the transit gateway with the Direct Connect gateway to provide secure communications from the company's data centers to the VPCs in us-east-1 and us-west-2.

Here's why this combination meets the requirements:

AWS Direct Connect: Provides a dedicated, high-bandwidth connection between the on-premises data center and AWS, ideal for transferring large amounts of data to S3.

Transit Gateway: Acts as a central hub for routing traffic between the on-premises data center (via Direct Connect) and VPCs in both us-east-1 and us-west-2 Regions.

Transit VIF: Connects the Direct Connect gateway to the transit gateway, allowing secure communication.

Direct Connect Gateway: Simplifies management by associating the Direct Connect connection with a single gateway for transit gateway routing.

Security: Direct Connect encrypts data in transit by default, adhering to the company's regulatory compliance needs.

Let's explore why other options are not ideal:

Option A: A private VIF can be used for Direct Connect, but using a Site-to-Site VPN over a VIF adds unnecessary complexity. Direct Connect itself encrypts data.

Option C: Using a single Direct Connect connection to both Regions limits scalability and might not be as fault-tolerant as a single connection to a transit gateway.

Option D: A public VIF is not recommended for production environments due to security concerns.

12) The most secure and compliant solution for transferring financial data to S3 in this scenario is:

B. Create an IPsec VPN connection over the transit VIF. Create a VPC and attach the VPC to the transit gateway. In the VPC, provision an interface VPC endpoint for Amazon S3. Use HTTPS for communication.

Here's why this option fulfills the requirements:

Direct Connect for Security: Leverages the existing secure and dedicated AWS Direct Connect connection for on-premises to AWS communication.

Transit Gateway Routing: Utilizes the transit gateway for centralized routing between the on-premises data center (via Direct Connect) and the VPC where the S3 interface endpoint resides.

VPC Interface Endpoint: Creates a private connection directly within the VPC to Amazon S3, eliminating the need for routing traffic over the public internet. This ensures compliance with the restriction on internet usage.

HTTPS for Encryption: Utilizes HTTPS for communication between the on-premises data center and the S3 interface endpoint, providing an additional layer of encryption for data in transit.

Let's see why other options are not ideal:

Option A: Using a public VIF for Direct Connect contradicts the requirement to avoid the public internet. Additionally, an IPsec VPN over a public VIF adds unnecessary complexity as Direct Connect itself encrypts data.

Option C: While creating a VPC and interface endpoint for S3 is partially correct, it misses leveraging the existing Direct Connect and transit gateway for secure on-premises connectivity.

Option D: Setting up an IPsec VPN over a public VIF and attaching directly to S3 exposes data to the public internet, violating the security requirement.

Therefore, Option B provides a secure, private, and compliant solution for transferring sensitive financial data to Amazon S3.

13) The most operationally efficient solution for verifying authorized customer requests in this scenario is:

C. Use an AWS Lambda@Edge function to inspect the authorized token inside the GET/POST request payload. Use the Lambda@Edge function also to insert a customized header to inform the web application of an authenticated customer request.

Here's why this option offers the best efficiency:

Lambda@Edge Integration: Lambda@Edge functions execute at the edge of the AWS network, closer to the user, minimizing latency compared to options involving the origin server (web application) or the load balancer.

Token Validation and Header Insertion: A single Lambda@Edge function can handle both tasks: inspecting the token for validity and adding a custom header to the request, streamlining the process.

Scalability and Cost-Effectiveness: Lambda@Edge functions are serverless, automatically scaling to meet demand and only incurring costs when invoked.

Let's explore why other options are less efficient:

Option A: ALB cannot natively inspect request payloads for token validation. While an ALB listener can insert headers, the validation logic would still require communication with the web application, adding latency.

Option B: While AWS WAF offers some inspection capabilities, it's not designed for complex token validation logic. Additionally, it wouldn't handle header insertion efficiently.

Option D: Creating and managing a separate EC2 instance with a third-party tool introduces additional infrastructure complexity and potential management overhead compared to a serverless Lambda@Edge function.

Therefore, Lambda@Edge offers a scalable, cost-effective, and low-latency solution for token validation and informing the web application about authorized requests.

Reference:

https://docs.aws.amazon.com/AmazonCloudFront/latest/DeveloperGuide/edge-functions.html

14) To establish connectivity between the staging VPC (VPC-B) in eu-west-2 and the on-premises data center in Dublin, the network engineer should implement a combination of the

following solutions:

B. Associate TGW-B with the Direct Connect gateway. Advertise the VPC-B CIDR block under the allowed prefixes.

D. Configure inter-Region transit gateway peering between TGW-A and TGW-B. Add the peering routes in the transit gateway route tables.

Here's why this combination achieves the desired connectivity:

Direct Connect Access: Associating TGW-B with the Direct Connect gateway allows VPC-B to leverage the existing secure connection to the on-premises data center.

Advertising VPC-B CIDR: Including the VPC-B CIDR block in the allowed prefixes on the Direct Connect gateway association informs AWS about the traffic destined for VPC-B.

Transit Gateway Peering: Establishing peering between TGW-A and TGW-B creates a private connection between the two Regions, enabling traffic routing between VPC-B and the on-premises data center via TGW-A.

Peering Routes: Adding peering routes in the transit gateway route tables guides traffic across the peering connection.

Let's see why other options are not ideal:

Option A: Inter-region VPC peering only connects VPCs within the same Region (VPC-A and VPC-B are in different Regions). Additionally, modifying the Direct Connect gateway association with VPC-B CIDR wouldn't provide connectivity through TGW-A.

Option C: While creating another transit VIF might be technically possible, it's unnecessary complexity as the existing Direct Connect connection can be leveraged by associating TGW-

B with it.

Option E: A Site-to-Site VPN connection wouldn't be the most efficient solution compared to leveraging the existing transit gateway infrastructure.

Therefore, using the existing Direct Connect gateway with TGW-B association and enabling inter-region transit gateway peering provides a secure and efficient way to connect the staging VPC in a different Region to the on-premises data center.

15) Correct answer: D. Create one dedicated connection. Use a transit VIF to connect to the transit gateway in us-east-1. Use a private VIF to connect to the VPC in eu-west-1. Use two Direct Connect gateways, one for each VIF, to route from the Direct Connect locations to the corresponding AWS Region along the path that has the lowest latency.

This option suggests using two Direct Connect gateways, one for each VIF, which aligns with the requirement of having separate connectivity for the VPCs in us-east-1 and eu-west-1. Therefore, Option D is indeed the correct choice.

References:

A and B are wrong, Direct Connect *hosted* connections only support 1 VIF per connection, see:

https://docs.aws.amazon.com/directconnect/latest/UserGuide/limits.html

C is wrong, see:

https://docs.aws.amazon.com/directconnect/latest/UserGuide/direct-connect-transit-gateways.html

> "You cannot attach a Direct Connect gateway to a transit gateway when the Direct Connect gateway is already associated with a virtual private gateway or is attached to a private virtual interface."

16) The most likely solution to the issue of EC2 instances not receiving responses from lengthy database queries after migrating to a NAT gateway is:

C. Enable TCP keepalive on the client EC2 instances with a value of less than 300 seconds.

Here's why this option addresses the problem:

NAT Gateway Timeout: NAT gateways have an idle timeout setting that terminates inactive connections. While increasing the timeout (Option A) might seem like a solution, it can lead to inefficient resource utilization and potential connection leaks.

Enhanced Networking: Enhanced networking (Option B) might improve overall network performance but wouldn't directly address the issue of dropped connections due to NAT gateway timeouts.

TCP Keepalive: Enabling TCP keepalive sends periodic packets from the client (EC2 instance) to the server (database) to verify the connection is still active. Setting the keepalive value to less than 300 seconds ensures these checks happen more frequently than the NAT gateway timeout, preventing the connection from being dropped prematurely. This allows the database to complete the lengthy query and send the response back to the EC2 instance.

Let's see why Option D is not ideal:

Closing Idle Connections: While closing idle connections (Option D) might free up resources in the NAT gateway, it could disrupt ongoing connections if the database query hasn't completed yet.

Therefore, enabling TCP keepalive with a value less than the NAT gateway timeout ensures connections are maintained even during lengthy queries, allowing the EC2 instances to receive responses from the database.

Problem

Your instances can access the internet, but the connection drops after 350 seconds.

Cause

If a connection that's using a NAT gateway is idle for 350 seconds or more, the connection times out.

When a connection times out, a NAT gateway returns an RST packet to any resources behind the NAT gateway that attempt to continue the connection (it does not send a FIN packet).

Solution

To prevent the connection from being dropped, you can initiate more traffic over the connection. Alternatively, you can enable TCP keepalive on the instance with a value less than 350 seconds.

When a TCP connection is idle for a long time, it may be terminated by network devices, including the NAT gateway. By enabling TCP keepalive, the client EC2 instances can periodically send packets to the third-party database to indicate that the connection is still active, preventing it from being terminated prematurely.

Reference:

https://docs.aws.amazon.com/vpc/latest/userguide/nat-gateway-troubleshooting.html#nat- gateway- troubleshooting-timeout

17) The user login issue likely stems from a lack of session persistence between the Application Load Balancer (ALB) and the EC2 instances in the production environment. Here's how the network engineer can address it:

C. Modify the ALB target group configuration by enabling the stickiness attribute. Use an application-based cookie. Set the duration to the maximum application session length.

Here's why this option effectively resolves the problem:

ALB Stickiness: Enabling stickiness on the ALB target group ensures that subsequent requests from the same user are routed to the same EC2 instance where they logged in. This prevents the application from restarting the login process for each request.

Application-Based Cookie: Selecting application-based cookie leverages the existing application session cookie mechanism to maintain session state. The ALB leverages this cookie to route the user back to the instance that holds their session information.

Maximum Session Length: Setting the duration to the maximum application session length guarantees that stickiness remains active for the entire user session, as defined by the application.

Let's explore why other options are not ideal:

Option A: Group-level stickiness might not be suitable if the application relies on session-specific data stored on the individual EC2 instance. Application-based cookie stickiness provides more granular control.

Option B: Replacing the ALB with a Network Load Balancer (NLB) is unnecessary. NLBs are not designed for application-level routing and SSL/TLS termination, which are already handled by the ALB effectively.

Option D: Removing the ALB and relying solely on Route 53 with failover routing wouldn't address the session persistence issue. Additionally, managing individual instance certificates with ACM would be less efficient compared to leveraging the ALB for centralized SSL/TLS termination.

Therefore, enabling application-based cookie stickiness on the ALB target group ensures users maintain their sessions and can navigate the application seamlessly.

Sticky sessions via the ALB are done via cookies. The source of the cookies can come from:

1) The application itself

2) Or the ALB

Reference:

https://docs.aws.amazon.com/elasticloadbalancing/latest/application/sticky-sessions.html

18) The most operationally efficient solution for detecting

malware distribution from EC2 instances with minimal additional configuration is:

A. Use Amazon GuardDuty to analyze traffic patterns by inspecting DNS requests and VPC flow logs.

Here's why this option offers the least operational effort:

Existing Service: Amazon GuardDuty is a managed threat detection service that already integrates with AWS services like EC2 and VPC.

Traffic Analysis: GuardDuty can analyze traffic patterns by examining DNS requests and VPC flow logs, potentially identifying suspicious outgoing traffic patterns that might indicate malware distribution.

Reduced Configuration: Leveraging an existing service with built-in analysis capabilities minimizes additional configuration and management overhead compared to deploying new security appliances or tools.

Let's see why other options require more operational effort:

Option B: While GuardDuty offers decoy deployment, it's not the most efficient solution for detecting malware distribution from existing compromised instances.

Option C: Setting up a Gateway Load Balancer (GLB) is unnecessary for inspecting traffic within a VPC. Additionally, managing and maintaining an intrusion detection system (IDS) on a separate EC2 instance adds complexity.

Option D: Configuring Amazon Inspector for deep packet inspection requires additional setup and potentially incurs higher processing overhead compared to leveraging GuardDuty's existing traffic analysis capabilities.

Therefore, utilizing Amazon GuardDuty's built-in traffic analysis features provides a low-effort solution for detecting potential malware distribution from compromised EC2 instances. It's important to note that GuardDuty might not be able to detect all types of malware, and additional security measures should be implemented for a comprehensive defense strategy.

This solution involves using Amazon GuardDuty to monitor network traffic and analyze DNS requests and VPC flow logs for suspicious activity. This will allow the company to identify when an application is spreading malware by monitoring the network traffic patterns associated with the instance. GuardDuty is a fully managed threat detection service that continuously monitors for malicious activity and unauthorized behavior in your AWS accounts and workloads. It requires minimal setup and configuration and can be integrated with other AWS services for automated remediation. This solution requires the least operational effort compared to the other options.

Reference:

https://aws.amazon.com/blogs/aws/new-for-amazon-guardduty-malware-detection-for-amazon-ebs-volumes/

19) The process of establishing a connection between a VPC in one account and a transit gateway in another account requires the account owning the transit gateway to share the resource with the account owning the VPC. Since auto-acceptance is disabled, manual acceptance is needed on the receiving end. Here's the correct sequence of steps:

D. 1. In the Connectivity account (owning the transit gateway):

Create a resource share in AWS Resource Access Manager for the transit gateway.

Provide the Production account ID.

Enable the feature to allow external accounts.

2. In the Production account (owning the VPC):

Accept the resource share invitation for the transit gateway.

3. In the Production account (owning the VPC):

Create an attachment on the transit gateway to the VPC subnets.

4. In the Connectivity account (owning the transit gateway):

Accept the attachment request for the VPC subnets.

5. In the Production account (owning the VPC):

Associate a route table with the attachment to define the routing path for traffic destined through the transit gateway.

Let's break down why this approach is correct:

Resource Sharing Initiation: The Connectivity account, which owns the transit gateway, needs to initiate the resource sharing process by creating a share in AWS RAM for the VPC in the Production account.

Acceptance by Production: The Production account must accept the shared resource invitation to gain access to the transit gateway.

Attachment Creation: Once the Production account has access, it can create an attachment on the transit gateway, specifying the VPC subnets that will connect.

Acceptance by Connectivity: The Connectivity account, owning the transit gateway, needs to accept the attachment request from the Production account.

Route Table Association: Finally, the Production account associates a route table with the attachment to define how traffic destined for specific routes will be directed through the transit gateway.

Following these steps ensures proper configuration and manual control over resource sharing and attachment acceptance.

Important Note:

This response addresses the scenario without auto-acceptance enabled. If auto-acceptance were enabled, steps 2 and 4 (manual acceptance) would not be necessary.

The transit gateway is owned by Connectivity account, and it is the production account who will create a VPC attachment to the TGW post resource share by Connectivity account through AWS RAM.

Reference:

https://repost.aws/knowledge-center/transit-gateway-sharing

20) Correct answer: C. Deploy the EC2 instances in the private subnets. Create an S3 gateway endpoint in the VPC. Specify the route table of the private subnets during endpoint creation to create routes to Amazon S3.

Placing the EC2 instances in the private subnets ensures they are not directly accessible from the internet.

Creating an S3 gateway endpoint in the VPC allows the EC2 instances to access Amazon S3 without going through the internet gateway or NAT gateway, reducing data transfer costs.

Specifying the route table of the private subnets during endpoint creation ensures that traffic destined for Amazon S3 is routed through the endpoint.

This approach meets the requirements of the scenario and minimizes data transfer costs by using the S3 gateway endpoint for S3 access.

Option C is the optimal solution as it involves deploying the EC2 instances in the private subnets, which provides additional security benefits. Additionally, creating an S3 gateway endpoint in the VPC will enable the EC2 instances to communicate with Amazon S3 directly, without incurring data transfer costs. This is because the S3 gateway endpoint uses Amazon's private network to transfer data between the VPC and S3, which is not charged for data transfer. Furthermore, specifying the route table of the private subnets during endpoint creation will create routes to Amazon S3, which is required for the EC2 instances to communicate with S3.

Reference:

Recurring questions about gateway VPC endpoints.

https://repost.aws/knowledge-center/vpc-reduce-nat-gateway-transfer-costs

21) The most secure and compliant solution to allow instance metadata access while adhering to the security team's restrictions is:

C. Outbound; Protocol tcp; Destination 169.254.169.254; Destination port 80

Here's why this option fulfills the requirements:

Outbound Traffic: The rule specifies outgoing traffic, allowing communication initiated by the EC2 instance itself to reach the instance metadata service.

TCP Protocol: The metadata service uses TCP for communication.

Destination: The destination is set to 169.254.169.254, the IP address of the instance metadata service.

Port 80: The destination port is set to 80, the default port used by the metadata service.

Let's see why other options are not ideal:

Option A & B: Inbound rules are not applicable here as the communication originates from the EC2 instance trying to reach the metadata service (internal AWS service).

Option D: Port 443 is typically used for HTTPS connections, while the instance metadata service uses port 80 (HTTP).

By following this recommendation, you can grant necessary access to the instance metadata service while maintaining a secure outbound-only communication channel as mandated by the security team.

Reference:

https://docs.aws.amazon.com/AWSEC2/latest/UserGuide/instancedata-data-retrieval.html

22) The most likely reason for the failure is:

C. The NAT gateway cannot allocate more ports.

Here's a breakdown of why this is the most probable cause and how to address it:

NAT Gateway Port Exhaustion: NAT gateways employ a pool of ephemeral ports to translate private IP addresses of application servers to public IP addresses for outbound internet traffic. When a large number of servers use the NAT gateway for frequent UDP probes, the port pool might become depleted, causing some servers to fail establishing connections.

UDP Protocol Support: While unlikely, it's worth noting that NAT gateways do indeed support UDP traffic. Option A can be ruled out.

Authentication Server Availability: Option B highlights the importance of verifying the availability of the authentication server itself, but it's less likely as the issue seems specific to a few servers.

NAT Gateway Subnet: Option D is incorrect because NAT gateways can reside in public subnets to facilitate internet connectivity.

Solutions to Address Port Exhaustion:

Increase the NAT Gateway Size: AWS offers different sizes of NAT gateways (small, medium, large) with varying capacities for ephemeral ports. Scaling up to a larger size may provide more available ports.

Implement Session Persistence (Optional): If applicable, consider configuring session persistence on the NAT gateway. This can help reuse established connections and reduce the frequency of port allocation for the same authentication server. However, session persistence might not be suitable for protocols like UDP, which are typically stateless.

Explore Alternative Approaches: Depending on your application's requirements, you could investigate alternative authentication mechanisms that don't require frequent outbound communication or involve dedicated instances for authentication purposes.

Additional Considerations:

Monitoring NAT Gateway Metrics: Continuously monitor NAT gateway metrics like active connections, ephemeral port utilization, and any potential errors to identify resource constraints and optimize your configuration.

Cost Optimization: If increasing NAT gateway size is necessary, weigh the cost implications against potential benefits and explore alternative approaches if cost becomes a significant concern.

By understanding NAT gateway port limitations and implementing appropriate solutions, you can ensure that your application servers successfully communicate with the authentication server using UDP probes.

Reference:

https://docs.aws.amazon.com/vpc/latest/userguide/vpc-nat-gateway.html#nat-gateway-basics

23) The most cost-effective connection option for the organization to set up initial testing with a storage gateway, considering their lack of existing AWS connectivity, is:

A. Use an internet connection.

Here's why this is the best choice for initial testing:

No Additional Setup Cost: Leveraging an existing internet connection avoids the need for additional setup fees associated with dedicated AWS services like VPN connections or Direct

Connect.

Simplified Configuration: Internet connectivity is readily available and requires minimal configuration compared to establishing VPN tunnels or managing Direct Connect links.

Initial Testing Needs: For initial testing purposes, the potentially lower bandwidth and security considerations of an internet connection might be acceptable. Data transfer costs for initial testing are likely to be minimal.

While other options offer benefits in specific scenarios, they are less suitable for this case:

Option B (VPN Connection): Setting up a VPN connection incurs additional configuration overhead and might involve subscription costs.

Option C & D (Direct Connect): Provisioning a Direct Connect private or public virtual interface is designed for dedicated, high-bandwidth connections to AWS. It's a more complex and expensive option for initial testing with a storage gateway.

Important Considerations:

Security: For production use after successful testing, consider establishing a secure connection like a VPN or Direct Connect to enhance data security when transferring sensitive organizational data to the AWS storage gateway.

Performance: If testing reveals performance limitations due to internet bandwidth, a more robust connection like a VPN or Direct Connect might be necessary.

Data Transfer Costs: While initial testing might incur minimal data transfer charges, be mindful of these costs if testing involves large data transfers.

By starting with an internet connection and considering security and performance requirements for production use, the organization can initiate cost-effective initial testing of their storage gateway and make informed decisions for future configurations.

If minimal cost is the most important point, AWS ingress internet traffic is free. Direct connect traffic is cheaper for outgoing traffic, but you'll pay a fix fee for the connection. An no VPN is needed as the backup software take care of the encryption, etc.

Reference:

https://docs.aws.amazon.com/storagegateway/latest/tgw/Resource_Ports.html

24) The action that will resolve the availability problem is:

B. Create a new subnet using a VPC secondary IPv4 CIDR, and associate an IPv6 CIDR. Include the new subnet in the Auto Scaling group.

Explanation:

The error message indicates that there are not enough available IPv4 addresses in the existing subnet to launch the instance. By creating a new subnet with a secondary IPv4 CIDR and associating an IPv6 CIDR with it, you can increase the available IPv4 addresses for your instances. Including this new subnet in the Auto Scaling group will ensure that instances are launched in this new subnet when needed, helping to alleviate the availability issues during peak load times.

25) The most straightforward solution to address the S3 connection timeouts with the least amount of effort is:

C. Update the application server's outbound security group to use the prefix-list for Amazon S3 in the same region.

Here's why this option offers the least effort and resolves the issue:

Efficient Update: Modifying the outbound security group for the application servers is a simple and localized change. It doesn't require complex scripting or additional infrastructure like Lambda functions or new VPC endpoints.

S3 Prefix List Alignment: Using the existing S3 prefix list ensures compatibility with the VPC endpoint and avoids the need to manage a separate set of IP addresses.

Let's explore why other options might involve more effort:

Option A: Implementing a Lambda function introduces additional complexity and ongoing maintenance for automated updates. It might be overkill for this specific scenario.

Option B: Updating VPC routing involves modifying route tables and might require additional troubleshooting if the initial configuration wasn't correct.

Option D: Creating a new VPC endpoint isn't necessary. The existing endpoint should be sufficient to handle the connections unless scalability limitations exist. Adding another endpoint adds complexity.

Additional Considerations:

Verify Security Group Rules: Double-check the security group rules to ensure they allow outbound traffic on the appropriate port (typically port 443 for HTTPS) to the S3 prefix list.

Monitor Connectivity: Monitor the connection attempts between application servers and S3 to identify any potential network issues beyond security groups.

By simply updating the outbound security groups to reference the S3 prefix list, the organization can likely resolve the connection timeouts efficiently and without introducing unnecessary complexity.

Reference:

https://docs.aws.amazon.com/vpc/latest/userguide/managed-prefix-lists.html

26) The most efficient design for the bank to serve both newer and older clients while phasing out the on-premises application is:

D. Use an Application Load Balancer (ALB) for the new application. Register both the new and earlier application backends as separate target groups. Use header-based routing to route traffic based on the application version.

Here's why this approach is optimal:

Application Load Balancer (ALB): An ALB is well-suited for modern applications that often leverage features like path-based routing and header-based routing.

Separate Target Groups: By registering both the new AWS-based application containers and the on-premises application instance as separate target groups, the ALB can differentiate between them based on routing rules.

Header-Based Routing: This method allows the ALB to inspect the HTTP headers in incoming client requests. Based on specific headers that identify the client version (e.g., "Client-Version"), the ALB can direct traffic to the appropriate target group (new version in AWS or older version on-premises).

Let's explore why other options are less efficient:

Option A: Amazon Route 53 multivalue answer routing is primarily for DNS record resolution and wouldn't be suitable for routing traffic based on application versions within the same domain.

Option B: Classic Load Balancer doesn't support user-agent based routing. Additionally, redirecting older clients to the on-premises application from the new application introduces unnecessary complexity.

Option C: Path-based routing typically relies on the URL path. It might not be the most effective way to differentiate between client versions unless the versions access distinct paths on the same backend.

Advantages of Header-Based Routing:

Flexibility: Header-based routing allows you to define custom headers within the client applications to identify their versions.

Scalability: As the bank phases out the older client version, the on-premises target group can be gradually removed, simplifying the infrastructure.

By implementing an ALB with header-based routing, the bank can efficiently serve both client versions while providing a seamless user experience. As the newer version adoption increases, the on-premises application can be decommissioned, further streamlining the infrastructure.

27) Correct answer: B. Deploy a Gateway Load Balancer with the firewall appliances as targets. Configure the firewall appliances with two network interfaces: one network interface in a private subnet and another network interface in a public subnet. Use the NAT functionality on the firewall appliances to send the traffic to the internet after inspection.

Two-arm mode: As shown in figure 5b below, the firewall is deployed in two-arm mode and performs both inspection as well as NAT. Some AWS partners provide firewall with NAT functionality. GWLB integrates seamlessly in such deployment mode. You don't need to do any additional configuration changes in the GWLB. However, the firewall networking differs – one network interface is on the private subnet and the other is on public subnet. This mode requires software support from the firewall partner. Some of the GWLB partners (Palo Alto Networks, Valtix) support this feature, however consult with an AWS partner of your choice before using this mode.

Based on the above, can we blindly choose two-arm or NAT functionality within the firewall for all third-party vendor appliances. Also, the cost of implementing firewall in two-arm mode for each appliance vs. cost of a single NAT gateway needs to be evaluated.

Firewall for "Traffic inspection" and "Nat capabilities" ==> Two arm mode.

28) Correct answer: B. Create a new Route 53 Resolver outbound endpoint in the shared services VPC. Create forwarding rules for the on-premises hosted domains. Associate the rules with the new Resolver endpoint and each application VPC.

Creating a new Route 53 Resolver outbound endpoint in the shared services VPC enables forwarding DNS queries from the VPC to on-premises DNS servers. Specifying forwarding rules for the on-premises hosted domains allows you to define which domain names are forwarded to the on-premises DNS servers. Associating these rules with the new Resolver endpoint and each application VPC ensures that the rules are applied to the VPCs. This approach does not alter the default DNS resolution behavior of Route 53 Resolver for local VPC domain names and domains hosted in Route 53 private hosted zones.

Should have been completed with DHCP Option set as AmazonProvidedDNS for resolving local VPC domain names.

29) The most operationally efficient solution for providing VPC and on-premises workloads with private access to S3 is:

C. Create an S3 interface endpoint. Configure an on-premises DNS resolver to resolve the S3 DNS names to the private IP addresses of the S3 interface endpoint. Use the S3 interface endpoint to access Amazon S3. Continue to use the S3 gateway endpoint for the VPC workloads to access Amazon S3.

Here's why this option offers the most operational efficiency:

Leveraging Existing VPC Endpoint: The S3 gateway endpoint remains in place for VPC workloads, maintaining their established connection method.

S3 Interface Endpoint for On-Premises: Creating an S3 interface endpoint facilitates private access to S3 for on-premises workloads via the VPN connection without requiring complex proxy configurations.

DNS Resolution: Configuring the on-premises DNS resolver to map S3 DNS names to the S3 interface endpoint's private IP addresses ensures proper routing for on-premises traffic.

Let's explore why other options are less operationally efficient:

Option A: Deploying and managing a proxy fleet with an ALB introduces additional complexity and ongoing maintenance overhead.

Option B: Deleting the S3 gateway endpoint disrupts the existing connection method for VPC workloads. Additionally, managing two separate endpoints (interface for on-premises, gateway for VPC) increases complexity.

Option D: Setting up a Direct Connect with a public VIF exposes S3 traffic to the public internet, introducing unnecessary security risks. Public VIFs are not typically recommended for S3 access.

Maintaining Separate Endpoints:

While seemingly redundant, maintaining separate endpoints for VPC workloads (S3 gateway) and on-premises workloads (S3 interface) might be strategically beneficial for:

Isolation: Separating traffic flows can simplify security group management and potential future access control requirements.

Performance Optimization: VPC workloads might benefit from the lower latency offered by the S3 gateway endpoint compared to the VPN connection used by on-premises workloads.

By combining the existing S3 gateway endpoint for VPC workloads with a newly created S3 interface endpoint for on-premises workloads, the company achieves efficient and secure private access to S3 for both sets of workloads while minimizing operational overhead.

30) To restore communication with AWS services using PrivateLink endpoints, the network engineer should focus on ensuring proper routing and policy configurations. Here are the two MOST suitable steps:

A. In the VPC route table, add a route that has the PrivateLink endpoints as the destination.

PrivateLink endpoints create a virtual interface within the VPC that serves as the entry point for traffic destined to the AWS service. Without a route in the VPC route table directing traffic to these endpoints, EC2 instances might not know where to send their requests.

C. Ensure that the VPC endpoint policy allows communication.

Each PrivateLink endpoint has an associated policy that specifies which AWS accounts and VPCs can access the service through the endpoint. If the policy is restrictive and doesn't include the current VPC or account ID, communication will be blocked.

Why other options are less relevant:

Option B (enableDnsSupport): While DNS support allows for hostname resolution of PrivateLink services, it's not strictly necessary for basic communication as long as the route table has the appropriate entries.

Option D (Route 53 public hosted zone): Public hosted zones are not required for PrivateLink, which operates within a VPC and doesn't involve public internet access.

Option E (Route 53 private hosted zone with custom names): While private hosted zones can be used for internal DNS resolution within a VPC, it's not directly critical for basic communication with PrivateLink services. It might be useful for custom service discovery within the VPC, but not essential for restoring initial communication.

By focusing on route table configuration and verifying the VPC endpoint policy, the network engineer can effectively re-establish communication between the EC2 instances and the desired AWS services using PrivateLink endpoints.

31) Correct answer: A. Configure a private hosted zone for each application VPC, and create the requisite records. Create a set of Amazon Route 53 Resolver inbound and outbound endpoints in an egress VPC. Define Route 53 Resolver rules to forward requests for the on-premises domains to the on-premises DNS resolver. Associate the application VPC private hosted zones with the egress VPC, and share the Route 53 Resolver rules with the application accounts by using AWS Resource Access Manager. Configure the on-premises DNS servers to forward the cloud domains to the Route 53 inbound endpoints.

Explanation:

Configuring a private hosted zone for each application VPC allows for end-to-end domain name resolution within AWS.

Creating Route 53 Resolver endpoints in an egress VPC enables bi-directional DNS resolution between AWS and the on-premises environment.

Defining Resolver rules to forward requests for on-premises domains ensures these requests are directed to the on-premises DNS resolver.

Associating the application VPC private hosted zones with the egress VPC and sharing the Resolver rules with the application accounts ensures all workloads have the necessary DNS resolution capabilities.

Configuring the on-premises DNS servers to forward cloud domains to the Route 53 inbound endpoints completes the bi-directional DNS resolution between AWS and the on-premises environment.

This option provides a comprehensive solution to the requirements of end-to-end domain name resolution and bi-directional DNS resolution between AWS and the on-premises environments during the migration of workloads.

PHZ cannot be shared, Route 53 resolver rules can be shared using AWS RAM.

32) The most suitable solution for the company's development account network monitoring and compliance needs is:

C. Record the current state of network resources by using AWS Config. Create rules that reflect the desired configuration settings. Set remediation for noncompliant resources.

Here's why this approach effectively addresses the requirements:

AWS Config: This service continuously monitors and records AWS resource configurations, including VPC network resources. It provides a historical record of changes, fulfilling the requirement to track configurations over time.

Compliance Rules: By creating AWS Config rules based on the company's network security policies, the system can automatically identify non-compliant resources when configurations deviate from the desired state.

Remediation: AWS Config can be configured to trigger automated remediation actions when non-compliance is detected. This helps maintain consistent security posture.

Let's explore why other options are less suitable:

Option A: While EventBridge and Lambda can be used for custom monitoring, relying on log analysis and building a custom solution might be less efficient than leveraging the built-in functionalities of AWS Config for network resource monitoring.

Option B: Similar to option A, custom CloudWatch metrics and Lambda functions create additional complexity compared to the pre-built capabilities of AWS Config for network resource configuration tracking.

Option D: While AWS Systems Manager Inventory can provide an inventory of resources, it doesn't offer the same level of configuration history and automated compliance enforcement as AWS Config. State Manager is more suited for configuration management and deployment, but not necessarily continuous monitoring and compliance checks.

Additional Considerations:

Alerting: Configure AWS Config to send alerts for non-compliant resources to notify the network engineer or security team.

Delivery Channels: Utilize AWS Config delivery channels to send configuration changes and notifications to Amazon SNS topics, S3 buckets, or CloudWatch Logs for further analysis or integration with other tools.

By implementing AWS Config with appropriate rules and remediation actions, the company can achieve efficient network resource change monitoring, strict compliance enforcement, and access to historical configurations within their development account.

33) The correct answer is:

D. Add an entry to the Network ACL outbound rules for Protocol: TCP, Port Range: 1024-65535

Explanation:

When accessing a web server from the internet, the inbound traffic on port 80 is indeed crucial. However, the response from the server back to the client also requires outbound rules to be set correctly. Here's why option D is the correct choice:

Security Group: Inbound traffic on port 80 is already allowed, but there's no outbound rule. Typically, security groups in AWS are stateful, meaning the return traffic (outbound) is automatically allowed. So, outbound rules in the security group are not necessary for this particular scenario.

Network ACL: Unlike security groups, Network ACLs are stateless. This means that for every rule you configure for incoming traffic, you must also configure a corresponding rule for outgoing traffic. The Network ACL only allows inbound traffic on port 80, and has no rules for outbound traffic. When the server tries to send the response back to the client, it uses a high port range (1024-65535). Therefore, you need to add an outbound rule to allow this return traffic.

Adding an entry to the Network ACL outbound rules for Protocol: TCP, Port Range: 1024-65535 ensures that the response traffic from the server to the client is allowed.

34) Correct answer: B. Create a new transit gateway in eu-central-1. Create a peering attachment request to the transit gateway in eu-west-2. Add a static route in the transit gateway route table in eu-central-1 to point to the transit gateway peering attachment. Accept the peering request. Add a static

route in the transit gateway route table in eu-west-2 to point to the new transit gateway peering attachment.

The best approach to connect resources in eu-central-1 to both the on-premises data center and resources in eu-west-2 while minimizing changes to the Direct Connect connection is by utilizing transit gateways.

Let's analyze the options:

A. This option utilizes a virtual private gateway (VGW) which is not ideal for VPC peering across regions. VGWs are typically used for internet connectivity.

B. This is the CORRECT approach. Transit gateways allow for central management of VPC peering connections across regions. By creating transit gateways in both regions and establishing a peering connection between them, resources in eu-central-1 can communicate with both the on-premises data center via Direct Connect and resources in eu-west-2 through the peered transit gateways. Static routes in the transit gateway route tables ensure proper routing.

C. While AWS Site-to-Site VPN can be used for VPC peering, it's generally less performant and more complex to manage compared to transit gateways for this scenario.

D. Public VIF on a Direct Connect connection wouldn't allow communication with the on-premises data center which is typically on a private network.

35) Correct answer: C

The most efficient and secure approach to connect the Tokyo workloads to the existing infrastructure in Paris while meeting the migration timeframe is by leveraging transit gateways and a

VPN connection.

Let's analyze the options:

A. This option creates public subnets, exposing workloads to the internet, which violates the requirement of no direct internet access.

B. This is a well-structured approach. It leverages transit gateways for centralized peering and utilizes a new Direct Connect connection for dedicated and secure connectivity between the Tokyo office and AWS. However, setting up a new Direct Connect might take longer than 5 days.

C. This is the MOST SUITABLE approach. It utilizes transit gateways for peering and leverages a VPN connection, which can be established quickly to meet the 5-day migration timeframe.

A VPN connection between the Tokyo office and the Tokyo transit gateway offers secure communication.

Peering connections between the transit gateways enable communication between workloads in Paris and Tokyo VPCs.

D. This option creates an association in the wrong direction. The peering needs to be established between the transit gateways, not associating the Tokyo VPC with the Paris transit gateway directly.

Therefore, the recommended steps for the network engineer are:

C. 1. Configure a transit gateway in the Asia Pacific (Tokyo) Region. Associate this transit gateway with the Tokyo VPC.

2. Configure an AWS Site-to-Site VPN connection from the Tokyo office. Set the Tokyo transit gateway as the target.

3. Create peering connections between the Tokyo transit gateway and the Paris transit gateway.

4. Configure routing on both transit gateways to allow data to flow between sites and the VPCs.

36) Correct answer: D. Create a VPC Reachability Analyzer path on port 443. Specify the internet gateway of the VPC as the source. Specify the EC2 instances as the destination. Create an Amazon Simple Notification Service (Amazon SNS) topic to notify the network engineer when a change to the security group affects the connection. Create an AWS Lambda function to start Reachability Analyzer and to publish a message to the SNS topic in case the analyses fail. Create an Amazon EventBridge (Amazon CloudWatch Events) rule to invoke the Lambda function when a change to the security group occurs.

Explanation:

Option D correctly addresses the requirements because:

Comprehensive Source Specification: By specifying the internet gateway as the source, the solution ensures that the entire path from the public internet to the EC2 instances is analyzed. This includes verifying that the internet gateway, route tables, and security groups are configured correctly to allow traffic.

Automatic Connectivity Verification: Using AWS VPC Reachability Analyzer provides a reliable method to automatically verify network paths whenever there is a change in the security group.

Automated Response: The AWS Lambda function is triggered by an EventBridge rule whenever there is a security group change, ensuring that the Reachability Analyzer is run automatically.

Proactive Notification: If the Reachability Analyzer detects any issues with the network path, the Lambda function publishes a message to the SNS topic, promptly notifying the network engineer about connectivity issues.

Option D ensures that any configuration changes impacting the network path from the internet gateway to the EC2 instances are detected and reported, providing a robust solution for maintaining the application's accessibility on port 443 from the public internet.

C is not correct because security group is not a valid source.

Reference:

https://aws.amazon.com/blogs/networking-and-content-delivery/automating-connectivity-assessments-with-vpc-reachability-analyzer/

37) Correct answer: B. Create an AWS Cloud WAN core network with an edge location in both Regions. Configure a segment for each BU with VPC attachments to the new BU VPCs. Use segment actions to control traffic between segments.

Explanation:

Operational Efficiency: Using AWS Cloud WAN allows for the creation of a core network with edge locations in both Regions, providing a centralized and efficient way to manage network connectivity.

Segmentation: By configuring a segment for each BU with VPC attachments to the new BU VPCs, you can effectively isolate and control traffic between BUs, meeting the requirement of isolating certain BUs from others.

Traffic Control: Using segment actions, you can control traffic between segments, ensuring that traffic flows as intended and meeting the requirement of controlling traffic between BUs.

Scalability: AWS Cloud WAN is designed to scale across multiple

Regions and BUs, making it suitable for accommodating future expansion.

Option B offers a scalable and efficient solution for managing network connectivity between multiple Regions and BUs while providing the necessary isolation and traffic control capabilities.

38) The correct answers are:

C. Resources:

newEC2Route:

Type: AWS::EC2::Route

E. Resources:

newVPCPeeringConnection:

Type: 'AWS::EC2::VPCPeeringConnection'

PeerRoleArn: !Ref PeerRoleArn

Explanation:

Option C:

When creating a VPC peering connection, you typically need to add a route to the route table of the Originating VPC to direct traffic destined for the Remote VPC to the VPC peering connection. This is achieved using an AWS::EC2::Route resource.

Option E:

The 'AWS::EC2::VPCPeeringConnection' resource defines the VPC peering connection itself. The 'PeerRoleArn' parameter, if used, specifies an IAM role in the Remote account that the Originating account can assume to manage the VPC peering connection. This parameter is optional but can be useful for cross-account peering.

References:

Creating the Role in CF template is below.

https://docs.aws.amazon.com/AWSCloudFormation/latest/
UserGuide/peer-with-vpc-in-another-account.html

A route table update is also required to make the new peering functional.

https://docs.aws.amazon.com/vpc/latest/peering/vpc-peering-routing.html

We need a role in peer account to accept the peer connection.

Then a route to route the traffic.

39) Correct answer: ABE

A. Create four virtual private gateways. Attach the virtual private gateways to the four VPCs.

B. Create a Direct Connect gateway. Associate the four virtual private gateways with the Direct Connect gateway.

E. Create four private VIFs on each Direct Connect connection to the Direct Connect gateway.

ABE are the correct answer as these are required to build the VPG setup.

CD are wrong due to the fact all the VPC will access the on-premises (you need to configure the 4 specific VPC prefixes in the DX gateway to TGW association or use different routing tables within the TGW to limit the routes to only the 4 VPCs required to access the on-premises)

F is not needed since VPG will be used.

Reference:

TGW for inter VPC peering within AWS. From on-prem access to only 4 VPCs is required. Hence DXGW and VGW via private VIF. Peering TGW with DXGW would be possible for on-prem connectivity but is more costly.

https://docs.aws.amazon.com/whitepapers/latest/hybrid-connectivity/aws-dx-dxgw-with-vgw-multi-regions-and-aws-public-peering.html

40) Correct answer: BE

B. Create a staging example.com NS record in the example.com domain. Populate the value with the name servers from the staging.example.com domain. Set the routing policy type to simple routing.

E. Create a public hosted zone for staging.example.com in the staging account.

When a client queries a DNS server for a domain name, the DNS server typically starts by looking for NS records to determine which name servers are authoritative for the domain. The DNS server then queries the authoritative name servers to obtain the information about the domain that the client requested.

For example, suppose you own the domain example.com, but you want to delegate control of the subdomain sub.example.com to a different set of name servers. You would create NS records in the example.com zone file that point to the name servers for sub.example.com. This tells DNS servers that the name servers for sub.example.com are authoritative for that subdomain, and they should query those name servers for any requests related to sub.example.com.

It is a case of sub-domain delegation, not split DNS.

Reference:

https://docs.aws.amazon.com/Route53/latest/
DeveloperGuide/CreatingNewSubdomain.html

41) Correct answer: C

The goal is to create a cost-effective solution for millions of IoT devices to connect to an application endpoint without DNS resolution.

Let's analyze the options:

A. Application Load Balancers (ALBs) are better suited for HTTP/HTTPS traffic, while Network Load Balancers (NLBs) handle TCP/UDP traffic commonly used by IoT devices. Additionally, attaching an Auto Scaling group to an ALB wouldn't provide the desired functionality.

B. This is a well-structured approach. AWS Global Accelerator offers static IP addresses that can be used by the IoT devices, eliminating the need for DNS resolution. An NLB at the endpoint handles distribution across the EC2 Auto Scaling group instances. However, using an ALB as the endpoint adds unnecessary overhead for an IoT application.

C. This is the MOST COST-EFFECTIVE approach. NLBs are optimized for TCP/UDP traffic and provide static IP addresses suitable for IoT devices. With an Auto Scaling group attached, the NLB distributes traffic across the instances efficiently. There's no need for the additional layer of an ALB in this scenario.

D. While using an NLB with Global Accelerator offers similar functionality to option C, it adds an extra layer (Global Accelerator) which might introduce additional costs for millions of connections.

Therefore, the most cost-effective solution is:

C. Use a Network Load Balancer (NLB). Create an EC2 Auto Scaling group. Attach the Auto Scaling group to the NLB. Set up the IoT devices to connect to the IP addresses of the NLB.

B, C, and D are also doable.

Let's think about the cost.

AWS Global Accelerator is definitely the best option, but it costs more money.

NLB is enough.

42) The correct answer is C. Create a new accelerator in AWS Global Accelerator. Add the ALB as an accelerator endpoint.

Explanation:

AWS Global Accelerator: This service is designed to improve the availability and performance of your applications for local and global users by directing traffic to optimal endpoints over the AWS global network. By adding the ALB as an accelerator endpoint, traffic from enterprise customers will be routed through the AWS global network to the ALB, reducing latency.

Network Load Balancer (NLB): NLB is used for extreme performance and is often used for TCP or UDP traffic where extreme performance is required. However, in this scenario, the requirement is to minimize latency for employees of enterprise customers, which can be better achieved with AWS Global Accelerator.

Amazon CloudFront: CloudFront is a content delivery network (CDN) service that accelerates the delivery of your websites, APIs, video content, and other web assets. It is not typically used for load balancing traffic to an application running on EC2 instances.

Amazon Route 53: Route 53 is a scalable domain name system (DNS) web service designed to route end users to Internet applications. While it can be used for routing traffic, it does not provide the same level of performance optimization for global applications as AWS Global Accelerator.

By using AWS Global Accelerator, the company can ensure that employees of enterprise customers can access the application with the least amount of latency, while also allowing the network engineer to configure firewalls to only allow outbound traffic to approved IP addresses.

Reference:

Statement to be noted - "The company must configure firewalls to allow outbound traffic to only approved IP addresses. The employees of the enterprise customers must be able to access the application with the least amount of latency."

While Cloudfront can provide low latency, given that the traffic will be routed to specified IPs, the scenario in this question leads to Global Accelerator – C

Global static IP - Simplify allowlisting in enterprise firewalling and IoT use cases.

https://aws.amazon.com/global-accelerator/

43) Correct answer: C. Create a central shared services VPIn the central shared services VPC, create interface VPC endpoints for Amazon S3 and Systems Manager to access. Ensure that private DNS is turned off. Connect all the VPCs to the central shared services VPC by using AWS Transit Gateway. Create an Amazon Route 53 private hosted zone with a full-service endpoint name for Amazon S3 and Systems Manager. Associate the private hosted zones with all the VPCs. Create an alias record in each private hosted zone with the full AWS service endpoint pointing to the interface VPC endpoint in the shared services VPC.

The goal is to consolidate access to Amazon S3 and Systems Manager for hundreds of VPCs with minimal operational overhead.

Let's analyze the options:

A. Central Egress VPC with Private NAT Gateways:

This creates a complex topology with hundreds of VPC Peering connections to the central VPC. Managing hundreds of peering connections would introduce significant operational overhead.

B. Central Shared Services VPC with Route 53 Forwarding Rules:

This is a good approach but requires managing hundreds of Route 53 forwarding rules, which can become cumbersome at scale.

C. Central Shared Services VPC with Private Hosted Zone and Alias Records:

This is the MOST SUITABLE approach with minimal overhead. Here's why:

It utilizes interface VPC endpoints for private access to S3 and Systems Manager within the central VPC.

Private hosted zones in each VPC eliminate the need for hundreds of individual Route 53 forwarding rules.

Alias records in the private hosted zones point to the interface VPC endpoints, simplifying DNS resolution.

Disabling private DNS on the interface VPC endpoints avoids potential conflicts with private DNS in individual VPCs.

D. Central Shared Services VPC with Public DNS on Endpoints:

Public DNS on interface VPC endpoints isn't recommended. It exposes service names to the VPC and requires enabling DNS support on Transit Gateway, adding complexity.

Therefore, using a central shared services VPC with private hosted zones and alias records offers the most manageable solution for hundreds of VPCs (Option C).

When you create a VPC endpoint to an AWS service, you can enable private DNS. When enabled, the setting creates an AWS managed Route 53 private hosted zone (PHZ) which enables the resolution of public AWS service endpoint to the private IP of the interface endpoint. The managed PHZ only works within the VPC with the interface endpoint.

In our setup, when we want spoke VPCs to be able to resolve VPC endpoint DNS hosted in a centralized VPC, the managed PHZ won't work.

To overcome this, disable the option that automatically creates the private DNS when an interface endpoint is created. Next, manually create a Route 53 PHZ and add an Alias record with the full AWS service endpoint name pointing to the interface endpoint, as shown in the following figure.

Reference:

https://aws.amazon.com/es/blogs/networking-and-content-delivery/centralized-dns-management-of-hybrid-cloud-with-amazon-route-53-and-aws-transit-gateway/

see Sharing PrivateLink endpoints between VPCs point.

44) Correct answer: D. Create one Amazon Route 53 private hosted zone for aws.example.com. Associate the private hosted zone with every VPC that has resources. In the private hosted zone, create DNS records for all resources.

Option D is the most appropriate because it involves creating a single private hosted zone for aws.example.com and associating it with every VPC that has resources. This ensures a centralized management approach.

With this approach, you can create DNS records for all resources within the private hosted zone, allowing for a consistent DNS suffix across VPCs and regions.

Options A, B, and C do not provide a centralized solution or are not suitable for achieving the desired outcome in a multi-VPC, multi-region environment.

It creates a single private hosted zone for aws.example.com. This ensures that all resources in all VPCs can be accessed using the same domain name.

It associates the private hosted zone with every VPC that has resources. This ensures that the DNS records for all resources are replicated to all VPCs.

It creates DNS records for all resources in the private hosted zone. This ensures that all resources can be resolved by DNS.

Option A is not a valid solution because it would create separate private hosted zones for each Region. This would make it difficult to manage DNS records and would not ensure that all resources are resolved under the same domain name.

Option B is not a valid solution because it does not apply the aws.example.com DNS suffix to all resources.

Option C is not a valid solution because it does not explicitly associate resources in different VPCs across multiple Regions with the aws.example.com domain name.

Single PHZ can be associated with VPCs across regions.

This blog is for multi-account DNS architecture, not region. Single PHZ can be associated with multiple VPCs across regions.

45) Correct answer: A

The goal is to reduce latency for employees in the London office accessing applications in the us-east-1 Region VPC. Let's analyze the options:

A. New Accelerated Site-to-Site VPN with Existing Transit Gateway:

This is the MOST SUITABLE approach. By enabling acceleration on the existing Site-to-Site VPN connection, traffic can leverage the AWS global network instead of the public internet, potentially reducing latency. Setting the transit gateway as the target gateway ensures traffic routes through the transit gateway for peering with other VPCs.

B. Modify Existing VPN without Acceleration:

While changing the target gateway to the transit gateway might improve routing for other VPCs, it wouldn't address the latency issue for the London office. Enabling acceleration is necessary for the performance boost.

C. New Transit Gateway in eu-west-2:

Creating a new transit gateway in London wouldn't directly improve the latency for accessing resources in the us-east-1 Region. It would add complexity without addressing the root cause.

D. Global Accelerator with VPN Endpoint:

Global Accelerator is primarily used for highly available public endpoints, not Site-to-Site VPN connections. It wouldn't provide the desired improvement and would introduce additional complexity.

Therefore, the most efficient solution is to modify the existing Site-to-Site VPN connection and enable acceleration, leveraging the AWS global network for faster traffic routing (Option A).

Reference:

https://docs.aws.amazon.com/vpn/latest/s2svpn/accelerated-vpn.html

46) The correct combination of steps for the network engineer to ensure that the client applications can resolve DNS for the interface endpoint is:

B. Create the interface endpoint for Amazon SQS with the option for private DNS names turned off.

C. Manually create a private hosted zone for sqs.us-east-1.amazonaws.com. Add necessary records that point to the interface endpoint. Associate the private hosted zones with other VPCs.

F. Access the SQS endpoint by using the private DNS name of the interface endpoint .sqs.us-east-1.vpce.amazonaws.com in VPCs and on premises.

Explanation:

B. By creating the interface endpoint for Amazon SQS with the option for private DNS names turned off, the endpoint will use public DNS names for resolution. This allows clients to resolve the endpoint's DNS name using public DNS.

C. Manually creating a private hosted zone for sqs.us-east-1.amazonaws.com and adding necessary records that point to the interface endpoint allows for customized DNS resolution for the endpoint. Associating this private hosted zone with other VPCs ensures that DNS queries for the endpoint are resolved correctly across the AWS environment.

F. Accessing the SQS endpoint using the private DNS name of the interface endpoint (.sqs.us-east-1.vpce.amazonaws.com) ensures that DNS queries for the endpoint are resolved internally within the VPCs and on premises, without relying on public DNS resolution.

Its internal and the access should be private, which makes F correct.

Reference:

aws.amazon.com/blogs/networking-and-content-delivery/centralize-access-using-vpc-interface-endpoints/

47) The correct answer is:

A. Set up an AWS Site-to-Site VPN connection between on-premises and AWS. Deploy an Amazon Route 53 Resolver outbound endpoint in the Region that is hosting the VPC.

Explanation:

Setting up an AWS Site-to-Site VPN connection between on-premises and AWS allows the EC2 instances in the VPC to communicate with on-premises servers. Deploying an Amazon Route 53 Resolver outbound endpoint in the Region hosting the VPC enables DNS resolution for on-premises servers from the EC2 instances.

Option B is incorrect because setting up an AWS Direct Connect connection with a private VIF and deploying Route 53 Resolver endpoints would involve more configuration and complexity than necessary.

Option C is incorrect because setting up an AWS Client VPN connection would be more complex than using a Site-to-Site VPN connection for this scenario.

Option D is incorrect because using a public VIF for Direct Connect and using the assigned IP address for connectivity to on-premises DNS servers would introduce unnecessary complexity and potential security risks.

Setting up an AWS Site-to-Site VPN connection between on premises and AWS would enable a secure and encrypted connection over the public internet1. Deploying an Amazon Route 53 Resolver outbound endpoint in the Region that is hosting the VPC would enable forwarding of DNS queries for on-premises servers to the on-premises DNS servers2. This would allow EC2 instances in the VPC to resolve names of on-premises servers during the migration period. After the migration period, the Route 53 Resolver outbound endpoint can be deleted with minimal configuration changes.

48) The correct answer is:

D. Configure an AWS Config rule to detect inconsistencies between the desired security group configuration and the current security group configuration. Create an AWS Systems Manager Automation runbook to remediate noncompliant security groups.

Explanation:

Option D provides a comprehensive solution to the problem. By configuring an AWS Config rule to detect inconsistencies in security group configurations, the network engineer can identify noncompliant changes. Using an AWS Systems Manager Automation runbook, the engineer can then automatically correct these noncompliant security group configurations. This solution helps prevent downtime by proactively detecting and remedying security group changes that could affect external access to the application.

Reference:

https://aws.amazon.com/blogs/mt/remediate-noncompliant-aws-config-rules-with-aws-systems-manager-automation-runbooks/

49) Correct answer: C. Configure VPC flow logs to be delivered into an Amazon S3 bucket. Use Amazon Athena to query the data and to filter for the port number that is used by the old protocol.

The objective is to verify application migration without causing downtime and identify instances still using the old protocol.

Let's analyze the options:

A. Amazon Inspector with Network Reachability Rules:

While Inspector can analyze instances for reachability, it might require some downtime for scanning and wouldn't provide real-time details of active connections.

B. Amazon GuardDuty with Filtering:

GuardDuty can offer insights into network traffic, but it wouldn't definitively identify applications using the old protocol. Filtering internet traffic might exclude legitimate uses of the same port as an ephemeral port.

C. VPC Flow Logs with Athena:

This is the MOST SUITABLE approach without causing downtime. Here's why:

VPC flow logs capture detailed information about network traffic within the VPC, including source and destination IP addresses, port numbers, and bytes transferred.

By querying the flow logs stored in an S3 bucket using Athena (serverless interactive query service), the network engineer can filter records based on the specific port number used by the old protocol.

This provides real-time insights into instances that might still be communicating using the outdated protocol.

D. Security Group Inspection and Removal:

While removing the old port from security groups could prevent further use of the protocol, it would introduce downtime if any applications still rely on it. This approach is risky for verification purposes.

Therefore, analyzing VPC flow logs with Athena offers a safe and efficient way to identify lingering instances using the old protocol without disrupting ongoing application functionality.

50) Correct answer: B. Create an Amazon Route 53 Resolver rule.

Associate the rule with the VPC. Configure the rule to forward DNS queries to the on-premises Windows DNS servers if the domain name matches example.internal.

Explanation:

The issue is related to DNS resolution within the VPC. By creating an Amazon Route 53 Resolver rule and associating it with the VPC, you can configure the rule to forward DNS queries for the example.internal domain to the on-premises Windows DNS servers. This will ensure that DNS queries for the internal API service are resolved correctly. Updating the hosts file or the /etc/resolv.conf file on the EC2 instance may solve the immediate problem but would not be a scalable or sustainable solution for all resources in the VPC. Associating a new DHCP options set with the VPC would also not address the DNS resolution issue.

51) Correct answer: C. Create a new prefix list. Add all allowed IP address ranges to the prefix list. Share the prefix list across different accounts using AWS Resource Access Manager (AWS RAM). Update security groups to reference the prefix list instead of individual IP address ranges. When a new partner is added, update the prefix list with the new IP address range. This solution avoids the need for multiple updates to security groups in different accounts, providing a centralized and efficient way to manage partner network IP address ranges.

Options A, B, and D involve using AWS Lambda functions to read and update IP address ranges and security groups, which introduces additional complexity compared to leveraging AWS RAM for centralized management. Therefore, Option C is the most operationally efficient solution.

Reference:

https://docs.aws.amazon.com/vpc/latest/userguide/managed-prefix-lists.html

52) Correct answer: D. Replace the existing 1 Gbps Direct Connect connection with two new 2 Gbps Direct Connect hosted connections. Create an AWS Client VPN endpoint in the application VPC. Instruct the remote employees to connect to the Client VPN endpoint. is the most cost-effective solution for the following reasons:

Bandwidth Increase and Cost Efficiency:

Doubles Bandwidth: Upgrading to two 2 Gbps hosted connections provides a total of 4 Gbps bandwidth, addressing the anticipated 20% increase (1.2 Gbps) and offering some room for future growth.

Lower Cost per Gbps: Hosted connections typically offer a lower cost per Gbps compared to dedicated connections, making this option more budget-friendly.

Remote Access and Scalability:

Client VPN: Client VPN scales efficiently for remote access compared to Site-to-Site VPN. Each remote user establishes their own connection, alleviating potential bottlenecks and performance issues associated with a single Site-to-Site VPN link.

Improved User Experience: Client VPN potentially improves performance for remote users by providing a more direct connection to the AWS environment compared to routing traffic through the on-premises data center.

Resiliency Enhancement:

Dual Direct Connect Connections: By having two separate Direct Connect connections, the company gains redundancy. If one connection experiences an outage, the other can continue to handle traffic, improving overall resiliency.

Comparison with Other Options:

Option A (New Dedicated Direct Connect): While it provides additional bandwidth, it's likely more expensive due to dedicated connection fees and potential LAG overhead, making it less cost-effective for the limited budget.

Option B (Site-to-Site VPN): Shifting traffic to a single Site-to-Site VPN could significantly impact performance due to potential bottlenecks and create a single point of failure.

Option C (Workspaces): Workspaces wouldn't address the overall bandwidth issue for both remote and on-premises users. Depending on usage, it could be costly.

Additional Considerations:

Continuously monitor traffic patterns to optimize bandwidth usage and identify any future scaling needs.

Explore AWS Global Accelerator for the new application if high availability for remote users is critical. This can further optimize access times for geographically dispersed users.

In conclusion, option D offers the most cost-effective solution by significantly increasing bandwidth, improving scalability and user experience for remote access, and enhancing overall resiliency with redundant connections, all within budget constraints.

53) Correct answer: C. Use AWS Network Manager Route Analyzer to analyze routes in the transit gateway route tables.

Verify that the VPC route tables are correct. Use VPC flow logs to analyze the IP traffic that security group rules and network ACL rules accept or reject in the VPC.

The goal is to troubleshoot connectivity issues between EC2 instances in different Regions connected via a transit gateway.

Let's analyze the options:

A. Network Manager + Flow Logs with Firewall Manager:

Network Manager is suitable for route analysis, but Firewall Manager isn't designed for analyzing VPC flow logs.

B. Network Manager + VPC Route Tables (correct option):

This approach is on the right track. Network Manager helps analyze routes in the transit gateway route tables, and verifying VPC route tables is crucial for proper routing.

C. Network Manager + VPC Flow Logs (best option):

This is the MOST SUITABLE approach for troubleshooting:

Network Manager analyzes routes within the transit gateway.

VPC flow logs provide detailed information about network traffic within the VPCs, including source and destination IP addresses, ports used, and accept/reject decisions based on security groups and network ACLs.

D. VPC Reachability Analyzer (not applicable):

VPC Reachability Analyzer is specific to a single VPC and wouldn't be helpful for inter-Region communication via transit gateway.

Justification for Option C:

By combining Network Manager and VPC flow logs, the network engineer gains valuable insights:

Network Manager: Identifies any routing issues within the transit gateway that might prevent communication between the Regions.

VPC Flow Logs: Reveal details about traffic flow within the VPCs, including whether security groups or network ACLs are blocking traffic for the specific communication attempt between the EC2 instances.

Analyzing these details together helps pinpoint the root cause of the connectivity issue, whether it's routing problems in the transit gateway or security group/network ACL misconfigurations in the VPCs.

54) Correct answer: ACF

A. Request a hosted connection from the APN Partner: This provides the dedicated bandwidth connection needed between the VPC and on-premises data center.

C. Create an AWS Site-to-Site VPN connection: This ensures that the data is encrypted in transit between the VPC and on-premises data center.

F. Create a public VIF: This allows the connection to be established between the VPC and on-premises data center.

You need public VIF in order to create a Site-to-Site VPN connection.

Private IP VPN is deployed on top of Transit VIFs, so it allows you to use AWS Transit Gateway for centralized management of customers' Virtual Private Clouds (VPCs) and connections to the on-premises networks in a more secured, private and scalable manner.

Request a hosted connection from the APN Partner (Choice A): This step involves requesting a dedicated connection, such as AWS Direct Connect, from the APN Partner. This connection provides the dedicated bandwidth needed for data transfer between the VPC and the on-premises data center.

Create an AWS Site-to-Site VPN connection (Choice C): This step involves setting up a Site-to-Site VPN connection between the VPC and the on-premises data center. This VPN connection ensures that data transferred between the VPC and the on-premises data center is encrypted in transit.

Create a public VIF (Choice F): This step involves creating a public Virtual Interface (VIF) for the Direct Connect connection. The public VIF allows the connection between the VPC and the on-premises data center to be established securely over the internet.

By combining these three steps, the company can meet its requirements for a dedicated bandwidth connection that is encrypted in transit between its VPC and on-premises data center, while also leveraging the expertise of an AWS Partner Network (APN) Partner for the setup and management of the connection.

Reference:

You need a public VIF because traditionally the VPN tunnels in S2S VPN use public IPs. However, since last year it is possible to use private IPs as well with a transit VIF.

https://aws.amazon.com/blogs/networking-and-content-delivery/introducing-aws-site-to-site-vpn-private-ip-vpns/

55) Correct answer: AC

A. Use an EC2 instance that supports enhanced networking.

C. Increase the EC2 instance size.

1) The security appliance runs on an Amazon EC2 instance.

2) Needs to improve the network performance between the on-premises data center and the security appliance.

Placement Groups is to allow better throughput between EC2 instances in your VPC. This does not improve throughput between the SINGULAR EC2 security appliance (security appliance runs on an Amazon EC2 instance) and on-prem DC. Therefore, increasing instance size (more vCPU/RAM) is the correct answer.

Using an EC2 instance that supports enhanced networking (A) can offload networking tasks to improve performance, and increasing the EC2 instance size (C) can provide more resources for processing and handling network traffic.

References:

Look at Table 1 and 2, last page of this document:

https://www.paloaltonetworks.com/apps/pan/public/downloadResource?pagePath=/content/pan/en_US/resources/datasheets/vm-series-spec-sheet

When you launch a new EC2 instance, the EC2 service attempts to place the instance in such a way that all of your instances are spread out across underlying hardware to minimize correlated failures. You can use placement groups to influence the placement of a group of interdependent instances to meet the needs of your workload.

Take a look on this:

https://docs.aws.amazon.com/AWSEC2/latest/UserGuide/placement-groups.html

56) Correct answer: B. In each Availability Zone in the VPC, create a subnet that uses part of the allowed IP address range. Create a private NAT gateway in each of the new subnets. Update the route tables that are associated with other subnets to route application traffic to the private NAT gateway in the corresponding Availability Zone. Add a route to the route table that is associated with the subnets of the private NAT gateways to send traffic destined for the application to the transit gateway.

The goal is to establish a highly available and compliant solution for Example Corp to access the on-premises application using the allocated IP address block (10.1.0.0/24) while adhering to their security requirements.

Let's analyze the options:

A. Public NAT Gateways in Each AZ (Not Ideal):

This creates a single point of failure if a public NAT gateway becomes unavailable in one AZ.

Public NAT gateways expose resources to the internet, potentially introducing unnecessary security risks.

B. Private NAT Gateways with AZ Redundancy (Preferred Approach):

This offers high availability with private NAT gateways in each AZ.

Private NAT gateways keep traffic within the VPC, aligning with compliance requirements.

C. Single Private NAT Gateway (Not Ideal):

A single private NAT gateway creates a bottleneck and reduces redundancy.

D. Public NAT Gateway with Transit Gateway Route (Not Ideal):

Similar to option A, this exposes resources to the internet and introduces security concerns.

Recommendation:

B. In each Availability Zone in the VPC, create a subnet that uses part of the allowed IP address range (10.1.0.0/24). Create a private NAT gateway in each of the new subnets. Update the route tables that are associated with other subnets to route application traffic to the private NAT gateway in the corresponding Availability Zone. Add a route to the route table that is associated with the subnets of the private NAT gateways to send traffic destined for the application to the transit gateway.

This approach provides a highly available and secure solution:

Redundant private NAT gateways in each AZ ensure application traffic can flow even if one gateway fails.

Private NAT gateways maintain compliance by keeping traffic within the VPC and not exposing it to the internet.

Route tables ensure traffic from other subnets is directed to the appropriate private NAT gateway based on Availability Zone.

A route in the private NAT gateway subnets directs traffic destined for the on-premises application to the transit gateway, enabling communication with AnyCompany's network.

The VPC uses the subnet 10.1.0.0/24 already. You cannot create a single subnet in that VPC range. Needs to be split up into multiple subnets.

"The network engineer starts by updating the VPC to add a new CIDR range of 10.1.0.0/24"

B is correct - Needs to be highly available so multiple AZ's required one in each of the 2 AZ's

"Example Corp has deployed a new application across two Availability Zones in a VPC with no internet gateway"

A and D - public NAT gateway has nothing to do here.

B provides a multi-az solution, compared to C.

Reference:

https://aws.amazon.com/blogs/networking-and-content-delivery/how-to-solve-private-ip-exhaustion-with-private-nat-solution/

57) Correct answer: A. AWS rotates the zone-signing key (ZSK). The company rotates the key-signing key (KSK).

Explanation: In DNSSEC, the zone-signing key (ZSK) is responsible for signing the resource records in a zone, and the key-signing key (KSK) is responsible for signing the ZSK. AWS Route 53 automates the rotation of the ZSK, while the company is responsible for rotating the KSK.

Reference:

You are responsible for KSK management, which includes rotating it if needed. ZSK management is performed by Route 53.

https://docs.aws.amazon.com/Route53/latest/DeveloperGuide/dns-configuring-dnssec.html

58) Correct answer: C. Place the EC2 instances in private subnets. Create an Amazon Route 53 private hosted zone for the AWS reserved domain name. Associate the private hosted zone with the VPC. Create a Route 53 Resolver inbound endpoint. Configure conditional forwarding in the on-premises DNS resolvers to forward all DNS queries for the AWS domain to the inbound endpoint IP address for Route 53 Resolver. In the private hosted zone, configure primary and failover records that point to the IP addresses of the EC2 instances. Create an Amazon CloudWatch metric and alarm to monitor the application's health. Set up a health check on the alarm for the primary application endpoint.

Route53 healthchecker need publicIP

References:

Can only be done using cloudwatch for private IPS

https://aws.amazon.com/blogs/networking-and-content-delivery/performing-route-53-health-checks-on-private-resources-in-a-vpc-with-aws-lambda-and-amazon-cloudwatch/

R53 cannot monitor pHz

https://repost.aws/questions/QUVcLK5gUqSxKGondJkrzw0Q/private-zone-route53-health-checks#:~:text=If%20you%20mean,private%20hosted%20zone

59) The correct answer is:

A. Add an inbound rule to the ALB's security group to allow the

AWS managed prefix list for CloudFront.

Here's why:

This approach achieves the desired outcome of restricting traffic to the ALB to originate only from CloudFront.

It operates at the network layer, filtering traffic based on source IP addresses, which aligns with the requirement for a network-based solution.

Using security groups is efficient because they are directly tied to the ALB and don't require modifications to multiple network ACLs.

The AWS managed prefix list for CloudFront simplifies configuration and ensures the rule stays up-to-date with CloudFront's ever-changing IP addresses.

The other options have drawbacks:

B. Network ACL Inbound Rule: While possible, it's less efficient as it might require changes to multiple ACLs.

C. CloudFront Custom HTTP Header: This adds complexity to the application layer and requires code modifications.

D. WAF Web ACL with CloudFront IP Set: WAF introduces unnecessary complexity compared to a simple security group rule for this specific purpose.

60) The most cost-effective way to meet the SLA requirement of 99.9% network uptime between the data center and AWS while ensuring redundancy and load balancing is option C: Add a second virtual interface (VIF) to the current Direct Connect connection and connect it to the existing VPC. Implement BGP for load balancing between the VIFs in active/active mode.

Explanation:

This option utilizes the existing 1 Gbps Direct Connect connection, avoiding the need to purchase additional connections or terminate existing connections.

Adding a second VIF provides redundancy and load balancing capabilities, ensuring that if one connection fails, traffic can be automatically rerouted to the other connection.

BGP (Border Gateway Protocol) is used for load balancing between the VIFs in active/active mode, ensuring efficient use of both connections.

This approach minimizes costs by leveraging the existing infrastructure and only adding the necessary components to meet the SLA requirement.

61) Correct answer: A. aggregate

Explanation:

AWS CloudTrail can be configured to aggregate log files across multiple accounts and regions so that log files are delivered to a single S3 bucket. This allows for centralized logging and easier management of logs for security and compliance purposes.

62) The appropriate services for storing session state data for a highly available web application using stateless web servers are:

D. DynamoDB

E. ElastiCache

Explanation:

DynamoDB is a fully managed NoSQL database service that can provide high-performance and scalable storage for session state data. It can handle large amounts of traffic and provide low-latency access to session data.

ElastiCache is a managed in-memory caching service that can be used to store session state data. It can help improve the performance of web applications by reducing the load on the backend database and providing faster access to frequently accessed session data.

CloudWatch (A) is a monitoring and logging service and is not suitable for storing session state data.

Storage Gateway (B) is a service that connects an on-premises software appliance with cloud-based storage, and it is not typically used for storing session state data.

Elastic Load Balancing (C) is a service that automatically distributes incoming application traffic across multiple targets, such as EC2 instances, and is not used for storing session state data.

63) Correct answer: C. Create an IAM role with permissions to access the table, and launch all instances with the new role.

Explanation:

Storing access keys in a text file on an AMI is not secure because anyone with access to the AMI can retrieve the keys.

Passing the access key through instance user data (A) or retrieving it from an S3 bucket (B) still involves storing the access key in a location that may not be secure.

Option D, obtaining the access key from a key server launched in a private subnet, could be a more secure option but would require additional setup and management.

The recommended and most secure solution is to create an IAM role with permissions to access the DynamoDB table and launch all instances with this IAM role (C). This way, the access key is not stored on the instances but is dynamically provided to the instances through the IAM role, which improves security.

64) Correct answer: A. Amazon Aurora

Explanation:

Amazon Aurora is a MySQL and PostgreSQL-compatible relational database built for the cloud, offering high availability and scalability.

Aurora can handle a database size of up to 64 TB per database cluster, which meets the initial storage capacity requirement of 8 TB and can accommodate the daily growth of 8 GB.

Aurora supports up to 15 read replicas per Aurora database cluster, which exceeds the requirement of at least eight read replicas for handling database reads.

DynamoDB (B) is a NoSQL database service and may not be suitable for a highly available relational database scenario.

Amazon S3 (C) is an object storage service and is not designed for relational database requirements.

Amazon Redshift (D) is a data warehousing solution and is not suitable for a highly available relational database with the specified requirements.

65) Correct answer: B. EBS Provisioned IOPS SSD

Explanation:

EBS Provisioned IOPS SSD volumes are designed to provide

predictable and high-performance storage for I/O-intensive workloads, such as databases.

Provisioned IOPS SSD volumes allow you to specify the IOPS (input/output operations per second) needed for your application, up to a maximum of 64,000 IOPS per volume.

EBS Throughput Optimized HDD (A) volumes are designed for frequently accessed, throughput-intensive workloads and may not provide the required IOPS performance.

EBS Cold HDD (C) volumes are designed for less frequently accessed workloads and do not offer the high IOPS performance required for this application.

EBS General Purpose SSD (D) volumes offer a balance of price and performance for a wide variety of workloads but may not provide the high IOPS performance required for this application.

Feel free to reach out to me anytime, and don't forget to connect with me on LinkedIn: <u>Georgio Daccache</u>. I'm always available to provide additional assistance and support.

Good Luck

www.ingramcontent.com/pod-product-compliance
Lightning Source LLC
LaVergne TN
LVHW052057060326
832903LV00061B/3092